PARTIES, DORMS
AND
SOCIAL NORMS

by the same authors

Helping Students with Autism Spectrum Disorder Express their Thoughts and Knowledge in Writing
Tips and Exercises for Developing Writing Skills
Elise Geither and Lisa Meeks
ISBN 978 1 84905 996 1
eISBN 978 0 85700 980 7

Independence, Social, and Study Strategies for Young Adults with Autism Spectrum Disorder
The BASICS College Curriculum
Michelle Rigler, Amy Rutherford and Emily Quinn
ISBN 978 1 84905 787 5
eISBN 978 1 78450 060 3

Developing Identity, Strengths, and Self-Perception for Young Adults with Autism Spectrum Disorder
The BASICS College Curriculum
Michelle Rigler, Amy Rutherford and Emily Quinn
ISBN 978 1 84905 797 4
eISBN 978 1 78450 095 5

Turning Skills and Strengths into Careers for Young Adults with Autism Spectrum Disorder
The BASICS College Curriculum
Michelle Rigler, Amy Rutherford and Emily Quinn
ISBN 978 1 84905 798 1
eISBN 978 1 78450 096 2

of related interest

Life on the Autism Spectrum
A Guide for Girls and Women
Karen McKibbin
Foreword by Tony Attwood
ISBN 978 1 84905 747 9
eISBN 978 1 78450 193 8

Decoding Dating
A Guide to the Unwritten Social Rules of Dating for Men with Asperger Syndrome (Autism Spectrum Disorder)
John Miller
ISBN 978 1 84905 780 6
eISBN 978 1 78450 040 5

PARTIES, DORMS AND SOCIAL NORMS

A CRASH COURSE IN SAFE LIVING FOR YOUNG ADULTS ON THE AUTISM SPECTRUM

**Lisa M. Meeks and Tracy Loye Masterson
with Michelle Rigler and Emily Quinn**

Forewords by Jane Thierfeld-Brown and Aaron Schatzman

Illustrated by Amy Rutherford

Jessica Kingsley *Publishers*
London and Philadelphia

First published in 2016
by Jessica Kingsley Publishers
73 Collier Street
London N1 9BE, UK
and
400 Market Street, Suite 400
Philadelphia, PA 19106, USA

www.jkp.com

Library of Congress Cataloging in Publication Data
A CIP catalog record for this book is available from the Library of Congress

British Library Cataloguing in Publication Data
A CIP catalogue record for this book is available from the British Library

ISBN 978 1 84905 746 2
eISBN 978 1 78450 192 1

Printed and bound in the United States

To my loves
Christopher, Layne Susan Sandra and Graham Kenneth Michael.
Also
In memory of my mother, Susan Loye.
Tracy

****

To my children
Kaitlyn and Christopher
You are my greatest joy.
To my amazing sister, Jeanine,
for helping improve the lives of children with autism.
And in celebration and memory of Ms. Etta James Jones,
my co-pilot on this project.
Lisa

This text is dedicated to the young adults and parents of young adults who shared their stories, their triumphs and their struggles to inform this book; thank you. Your guidance and experiences will help others safely navigate the transition into adulthood.

*****

From the authors
To all the teachers, therapists, behavior analyst and organizations who dedicate their resources to working with individuals on the spectrum—you are angels.

Contents

Acknowledgments

The authors wish to acknowledge the contributions of the following individuals:

- Lisa Clark, Editor, Jessica Kingsley Publishers
- Suzanne Connelly, Editorial Assistant, Jessica Kingsley Publishers
- Emma Katharine Dargen, Research Assistant for Dr. Meeks, UC Berkeley
- Taylor M. Hanes, Research Assistant for Dr. Masterson, John Carroll University
- Patricia Zentner, Research Assistant for Dr. Masterson, John Carroll University
- Nathaniel L. Jones, Editor, Cleveland, OH
- Milestones Autism Resources, Cleveland, OH
- Emily McClave, Original and Former Commissioning Editor, Jessica Kingsley Publishers
- Dr. Jane Thierfeld-Brown, College Autism Spectrum
- Beth Thompson, Teen/Adult Services Manager, Milestones Autism Resources
- All of the families and young adults who graciously shared their stories about safety.

Foreword

A Parent's Perspective

The title of Eli Gottlieb's recent *The New York Times* article, "Adult, autistic and ignored" (September 5, 2015) encapsulates the desperation of most parents and family members who live with or love an adult on the spectrum. For too long, authors, service providers, researchers and programs have focused on children with autism and left the adults with no services and little hope for supports outside their families. As a service provider, researcher and parent, I was often alone in banging the drum for adults on the spectrum. In the 1990s and early 2000s I was one of a handful of speakers talking about adults at national autism conferences, one of a small group of speakers defending monies for adult programs compared with hundreds of people championing children with autism. If I was frustrated, how did the young adults on the spectrum feel?

In the 15 to 20 years since that time some services and programs have begun to address adult issues but much more needs to be done. In the year 2000, the US higher education system had only one or two college programs for students with autism. This academic year (2015–2016), there will be closer to 30 programs and enhanced services for students on the spectrum pursuing college degrees. Additionally, vocational training programs are being developed and the healthcare system is looking to improve the delivery of medical care to adults on the spectrum. However, these areas need to be vastly increased in order to address what the Centers for Disease

Control and Prevention state is the 500,000 people on the spectrum that will be adults by 2020.

Besides education and healthcare concerns, people on the spectrum have serious challenges with employment and housing. However, it is not possible to address any of these issues without recognizing the need for independence and safety. Adults on the spectrum cannot work and live independently without learning skills for safely navigating the adult world.

The authors understand the broader issues of young adults on the spectrum and have written a volume that focuses on the need for independence and safety. Through the use of charts, guidelines and summaries, the authors convey critical information in a clear, concise manner. This book provides organized, specific advice that young adults can use as a resource. For example, many young adults with autism are hesitant to discuss highly personal topics (dating, drinking, sex and socializing). The authors provide this information in a reader-friendly, accessible format where young adults can gain knowledge in great detail while maintaining privacy and self-respect.

The authors are respectful and informative, explaining concepts that may be socially confusing and cloaked in non-verbal cues for young adults on the spectrum. This manual fills a gap in resources and for that we parents and young adults on the spectrum are grateful.

Jane Thierfeld-Brown, Ed.D.
Director, College Autism Spectrum,
Assistant Clinical Professor,
Yale Child Study, Yale University

Foreword

A Young Adult's Perspective

As a young adult living on the spectrum, there are many unforeseen social nuances that affect everyday life. Things like keeping a watchful eye on surroundings and being able to effectively judge the boundaries of a relationship are examples of social norms that are often innate for neuro-typical interactions, however, for those with autism spectrum disorder (ASD), they can be difficult to remember while also tending to our physical well-being. For those who are on the higher functioning end of the scale, these challenges can often be overshadowed by our accomplishments or abilities. We may not receive the same guidance associated with individuals who *seem to be* more at risk or vulnerable.

I have personally been on the receiving end of many lectures about personal safety and conduct and also learned some hard lessons on my own. Many times I have found myself at the crossroads of "if only I knew" and "if someone just told me." I have to remind myself that those things like locking up when I leave are not like needing to be reminded to inhale and exhale. Luckily, I've had a strong support network growing up and while faced with enormous challenges (many self-inflicted), I've made it through life largely intact.

Throughout this book, the authors, myself and many other contributors work to translate the safety concerns of the "typical" world into a context that may be easier to digest and process for young adults on the spectrum, with a focus on increasing the benefits of social connectivity as safely and effectively as possible. Sensitive and hard-to-discuss issues (often glossed over for individuals with ASD), such as dating, measuring the stages of relationships, sex and drinking, are covered frankly, bluntly and thoroughly. While of the utmost importance to everyone, these tough discussions affect young adults on the spectrum differently, oftentimes due to the awkwardness of the topic and the social faux pas that happen during everyday spectrum living.

Furthermore, this text encompasses as many of these life lessons in a relatable, easy-to-use format for individuals who are on the spectrum, breaking down complex interactions and safety-oriented situations into visual and queue-based guides with guidance that offers both insight and pathways into a world that can be difficult to process. It also provides additional dialogue and customized support from parents or professionals in the field.

What the authors have done is taken a lot of the guesswork and implications out of everyday life situations and emergencies, and outlined steps and plans of action that are easy to remember and apply.

Aaron Schatzman

PART ONE

Social Aspects of Adult Life

Chapter 1

Socializing Safely

What would happen if the autism gene was eliminated from the gene pool? You would have a bunch of people standing around in a cave, chatting and socializing and not getting anything done.

Temple Grandin

TOP SAFETY CONCERNS

★ Making friends and meeting people.

★ Socialization rules.

★ Transportation issues.

★ Feeling safe at the pub/club/party.

★ Meeting people and exchanging contact information.

Navigating the Social Jungle

Learning how to navigate common social scenarios including parties, social events, bars and clubs is an important skill and one that can be intimidating for young adults on the spectrum. Attending a social event is complicated, with many factors to consider. You may prefer to minimize exposure to social events to avoid overstimulation, or you may want to increase your social interactions but struggle with knowing how to manage these complex situations and the associated safety concerns (e.g., avoiding social blunders, meeting new people and making friends, etc.). This chapter will discuss topics relevant to socializing and navigating the social jungle and can serve as a guide for developing and practicing the skills necessary for *safe* socialization (see figure "Impact of socialization on young adults with ASD").

> When I go out to a social event, it's important for me to know the exact details of the event. Because of my personality and the fact that I have ASD, I like to know the exact time of the event, who is going to be there, and what activities will occur before I go. An individual who is not on the spectrum may not need to know these exact details, but it helps reduce anxiety for individuals on the spectrum to have information. In order for me to have a sense of safety when attending a social event, it is important for me to know who to call if I want to leave the event. It may be beneficial to discuss ahead of time "what to do if I want to leave" or "what to do if I feel uncomfortable." (Olivia, young adult with ASD)

Socializing and the Need for Socialization

Deciphering the *unwritten* rules of socialization is challenging for individuals on the spectrum and can lead to safety concerns. You may have experienced difficulties with the subtle rules of interacting with others, particularly because these "rules" are subject to change depending on the situation or the people involved. Understanding these social rules and their nuances is the gateway to developing friendships, romantic relationships and work/academic connections, and navigating everyday life; therefore, it is important that you practice and understand social skills that will you help you socialize safely in a variety of situations.

The following four rules of social engagement, adapted from *Developing Identity, Strengths, and Self-Perception for Young Adults with Autism Spectrum Disorder*,[1] are helpful in a multitude of social situations. Approaching social interactions with these rules in mind will help you acheive greater social success.

The Rules

1. **First impressions are vital**: You never know how important a person could be in your life. The impression you leave in your initial interaction could frame your future interactions with that person. You almost never get an opportunity to make a new first impression, so make sure you do it right the first time!

2. **Manners matter**: Instead of treating others as you would like to be treated, which can get confusing, perhaps a better rule is to always use good manners. Respectful and considerate behaviors include: saying please and thank you, apologizing if you offend someone, not interrupting others, not touching anyone or their belongings without permission and allowing others personal space. However, good social manners also include having an awareness of acceptable behavior in public versus in private (e.g., how you sit, what you wear, how you talk).

3. **People behave differently in different situations**: You likely enjoy consistency in life, however, when it comes to dealing with people, the rules often change from one situation to another. Depending on *where you are*

---

1   Rigler, Rutherford and Quinn (2015)

(at work versus school versus in your home) or *who you are with* (a supervisor versus a sibling versus a romantic partner) and your level of comfort with the person, you have to alter your behavior to be socially appropriate. For example, you would not behave the same way with a coworker as you would with your boss. Learning how to interpret and execute which behaviors are acceptable in different settings and with different people may take some planning and processing, but it is worth it; failure to understand these slight changes may put you in an uncomfortable minefield of social errors.

4. **Relationships are dynamic**: Perhaps one of the most difficult rules of socializing deals directly with the changes that naturally occur in relationships. Relationships are continually defined and redefined, and with this comes a change in expectations. You may have a difficult time understanding how to make the shift in social requirements based on the type of relationship. Someone who you may have initially thought of as a boyfriend/girlfriend could easily shift back to the status of friend. By defining potential social roles and the social expectations associated with each of those roles, you can gain a stronger grasp of the expectations and practice using them in various situations. It is especially important that you clarify the relationship roles and expectations when something about the relationships changes (e.g., changing from a friendship to a romantic relationship).

As Rule 1 says, the impression you leave in your initial interaction could frame your future interactions with that person. Making a good first impression is, therefore, extremely important. See "First impressions are vital," which offers advice for making a good impression and warnings about behaviors that may leave a bad impression.

18

Making a good impression	Making a bad impression
Smiles/happy face	Frowning
Acknowledging others	Ignoring or avoiding interaction
Tidy appearance	Disheveled appearance
Showing good manners	Lack of good manners
Greeting	Interrupting
Eye contact	Limited eye contact
Investing in balanced conversation	Dominating conversations
Honesty	Deceitfulness

First impressions are vital

What Type of Socialization is Right for Me?

Jordan does not like parties, even smaller family parties. When we do socialize with family, it is important for Jordan to have access to his trampoline to give him a sensory break, have a safe space in the house for him to decompress, and to prepare him well for the social event. For gatherings with family not at our home, Jordan would mostly seek out a place where he could be with-but-apart-from the commotion (i.e., wander from room to room and withdraw mentally). While he has several same-aged cousins, I've noticed that he seems to interact best with adults, so I no longer push him to "hang out" with his cousins unless he initiates it. Because Jordan has less insight about his behavior in social situations, we've benefitted from observing his behaviors, social successes and social challenges to help structure these events. (Jordan's Mom, Jordan is a young adult with ASD)

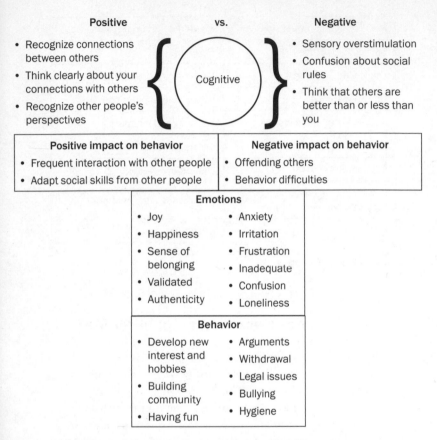

Positive   **vs.**   **Negative**

Positive (Cognitive):
- Recognize connections between others
- Think clearly about your connections with others
- Recognize other people's perspectives

Negative (Cognitive):
- Sensory overstimulation
- Confusion about social rules
- Think that others are better than or less than you

Positive impact on behavior	Negative impact on behavior
• Frequent interaction with other people • Adapt social skills from other people	• Offending others • Behavior difficulties

Emotions

• Joy	• Anxiety
• Happiness	• Irritation
• Sense of belonging	• Frustration
	• Inadequate
• Validated	• Confusion
• Authenticity	• Loneliness

Behavior

• Develop new interest and hobbies	• Arguments
	• Withdrawal
	• Legal issues
• Building community	• Bullying
• Having fun	• Hygiene

Impact of socialization on young adults with ASD

Everyone has individual preferences when it comes to socializing. You might prefer small group events or love the excitement of being out on the town. For those who prefer smaller events (two or three people), it is possible to avoid large outings such as concerts, bars/clubs and parties. However, it is much harder to avoid larger events that are considered non-optional yet have similar social demands and stressors such as a wedding, bar/bat mitzvahs or birthday parties. The guiding principles in this chapter, while directed to social events outside of the family, can also be used to help you reduce your stress and anxiety during family-oriented events.

You may or may not have a limited interest in going to clubs, parties and bars for a variety of reasons. Some young adults feel that the sensory overload from noise, crowds and smells in combination with high social demands are too stressful and not worth the effort and potential consequences of stress, overstimulation and anxiety. Whether or not you want to pursue socializing at parties, clubs or other organizations will depend on your interests and your ability to adapt your individual needs to the situation.

Impacts on Socialization

- Interest in socializing in these arenas.
- Social skill level.
- Adaptive skills (e.g., money management, navigational skills, independence).
- Coping skills/sensory sensitivities.
- Your prior experience in social situations.
- Amount of freedom and responsibility given by your parents/guardians.
- Access to transportation and money.
- Your knowledge of alcohol and drug-related issues.

Connecting Safely: Meeting New People

Part of the appeal of socializing and attending events is the chance for you to meet new people. Figuring out who is trustworthy can be very difficult but it is an important skill for socializing successfully and safely.

Considerations When Meeting New People at a Social Event

- **Beware of anyone asking you too many personal questions** (e.g., about your address, credit card numbers, how much money you make). By telling someone too much information, you are jeopardizing your safety.

- **Avoid asking someone else too much personal information**, as it is likely to make the person you are talking to uncomfortable. Good topics of initial conversations include current events, hobbies, musical interests and/or general info about their job or area of study.

- **Use caution with location and transportation**. Do not go in a car or to the home of someone you do not know well. Also, be sure to stay in public, well-lit areas as much as possible and try to avoid isolated areas (e.g., parking lots, alleys, etc.). If you do have to walk in dark or confined areas, make sure to go as a group.

- **Stick together.** Use the buddy system by maintaining close physical proximity to trusted friends (the buddy system involves pairing up with a friend and keeping an eye on each other).

If making friends is a struggle for you, it may be beneficial to try and locate people with common interests at your school or workplace or within your local community. You are likely to have a more enjoyable time when socializing with friends who share similar interests. Remember that making new friends is a process and takes time. Relationships need time to develop, allowing you and the other person to get to know each other as a potential friend. Over time you will be able to determine if others are honest, trustworthy and well intentioned.

Finally, not all friendships develop in person. Many individuals find success in establishing online social relationships based on shared activities and the desire for interpersonal interaction.

> Meeting friends in online games/chat rooms began at 16 years of age and has been a very positive experience for Hikarih. It has been an opportunity to socialize in a way that she is "all in" and provides her lots of joy. For example, Hikarih had a Halloween party in the world of one of her games with her online friends. They dressed the characters in costumes, "decorated" the rooms in their online world and planned it for weeks. On the night of the actual online party, because of the chatter, talking and laughter (they all have microphones and headsets) it sounded like a really party in her room. It was noisy and exciting and joyful—it reminded me of a teen prepping for the prom. However, after 45 minutes, Hikarih closed the computer and was done—this was a really safe way for her to end a social interaction. Exiting a more traditional social interaction is very complex. (Hikarih's mom, Hikarih is a young adult with ASD)

Connecting Safely: Socializing via Social Media

You may find success in connecting with others through social media. For safety reasons, it is critical that you only befriend people you know personally or who have earned your trust over time. It is also unwise to disclose where you are or what you are doing on social media, especially in real time. Individuals interested in burglarizing one's home or locating someone when they are not with their family could gain information from such posts. For example, if you "check-in" on social media that you are at Comic Con in Las Vegas with your family, this is alerting everyone in your friends list and possibly friends of friends that your home is vacant (see Tip 1.1).

TIP 1.1 Safety considerations when meeting new people

☑ **Do not give out personal information** like your address or last name right away. Note: emails that contain identifiable information like your last name may not be wise to exchange with someone you just met.

☑ **Keep a general voicemail**. If you are interested in maintaining contact, giving a phone number may be acceptable, because if they do call or text, you have more control about whether or not you talk with them. Be sure, however, to keep a generic voicemail or include only your first name (i.e., "Hi, this is Jenny. Please leave a message" compared to "Hi, this is Jenny Jacobs. Please leave a message").

☑ **Ensure that your social media does not have identifiers**. Make sure social media does not include personal information, date of birth, phone number or address. This way you can maintain casual friendships and connect with people via social media and reduce safety issues.

☑ **Avoid posting extensive personal or revealing information on your social media outlets** (i.e., no addresses or pictures of your house/apartment). Deciding whether to put the specific name of the school you attend or your place of work may depend on the size of your school or company and the level of security at school or work. You should also be discerning about the type and number of pictures you have on social media. Also, make sure you maintain security settings that give you control over who sees your profile.

☑ **Utilize thoughtful and stringent security settings on social media** (i.e., letting only "friends" see your posts, as opposed to "friends of friends").

See more information on internet safety in Chapter 4.

Meeting People: Where to Go

It is important to realize that finding people to go out with and/or meeting new people in social settings can be challenging for everyone—not just for people with autism spectrum disorders (ASD). While you may have an existing group of friends and plenty of opportunities to socialize, you also may find that making friends and meeting new people can be a major challenge, especially in a new situation.

> We [individuals with ASD] never know where to go, especially if we are alone. Even with a friend, sometimes I panic if I don't know anyone or have someone to talk to. I think it is good to take a buddy that understands your strengths and weaknesses. A good friend can help pull you into a conversation. (Alex, young adult with ASD)

So how do you safely make new friends? Having a trusted friend or family member is an excellent way to keep safe and, as suggested by Alex, these folks can help you determine a good location for socializing. If you have siblings or cousins who are close in age (and with whom you feel comfortable), socializing or "going out" with them may be a good starting point. Many young adults on the spectrum do not have a safe and established peer group to hang out with, so thinking about safe ways to meet people is important.

Organizations and Clubs

> If you have an interest in it there is a convention for it. I have an extreme interest in amusement parks and I found out that there is a convention for that. These are registered, organized events for people with similar interests. Have a friend come with you that enjoys sharing that topic to the LEVEL you like it. You can burn people out if your interest in the topic is very different from theirs. There are organized groups as well. Stick to organized events—you know that it is legitimate and that there is security, if it's in a more organized environment. (Aaron, young adult with ASD)

Meeting people through shared interests and clubs is a great idea as long as you take precautions to ensure that the club or organization is legitimate. Finding organizations to join through trusted friends or family members or from others who share your interest is a good place to begin. Of course, going with a friend or family member to the first meeting or event is also a wise decision. To ensure that the organization is credible, it is wise to investigate the organization online prior to going to the first meeting.

Ensuring an Organization is Credible

Most clubs or organizations have an established webpage with detailed information. Additionally, a local organization or club may be associated with a larger national organization that can provide you with information on the group and serve as confirmation of the group's legitimacy. The website is also likely to tell you how organized, active or current the group is. If the information is current and up to date, there is a good chance that the group is active and may have upcoming events. You don't want to set yourself up for disappointment by finding and joining a group that rarely sponsors planned events. You should always attend an event or meeting as a guest before committing to the organization. If they do not allow you to "sample" the organization before joining, that may be a red flag. Further, a club or group that has meetings in a public location, as opposed to someone's house or isolated location, is always a safer choice (see Tip 1.2).

> It might be a warning sign if members of a club or organization were making me do unnecessary work or stupid crazy things like making me get food for them with my own money and treating me as inferior. Definitely using my money to gain membership is a warning sign. (Liam, young adult with ASD)

TIP 1.2 Factors to examine before committing to a club or organization

☑ How long the organization has been established.

☑ Group member lists if available.

☑ Leadership structure for the organization.

☑ Membership fees and obligations.

☑ Other group affiliations (such as a national organization).

☑ Location and typical hours of meetings and events.

☑ Types of meetings and events.

I would look at the length of time they've been established if they haven't been around long, be cautious. See who/what the group is affiliated with. Look for the names of people who are involved in the field that you are excited to meet. Look for familiar items, friends, organizations. Also Google it—see what other people say and what people who have attended in the past have to say. Google Street View can assist with determining if it's a shady place. (Aaron, young adult with ASD)

TIP 1.3 **Safety considerations for joining organizations**

☑ Do your research—check the website for information and recent events.

☑ Check to see if they are affiliated with a national organization.

☑ Ensure they meet in a public place.

☑ Don't pay dues or give other monies until you are certain you want to join.

☑ Make sure they offer a trial of membership.

☑ Ask around—see if others are familiar with the group.

It is also possible to start your own group or club if you know of several people who share your interests. Ideally, forming a club with individuals who all have different skills is useful (e.g., a person to market or advertise events, a socially savvy person, someone skilled with money management, etc.). As the organizer of the group or club, you'll have responsibilities that may require that you interact with most, if not all, members. As such, leadership positions within these organizations can provide structure and support your socialization. Being part of a team, in a leadership position or as a member, can promote your sense of inclusion in a social setting that interests you.

Safety in Shared Experiences: ASD or Shared Interest Focused Events

> Hikarih did not want to go to the social skills group facilitated by her mental health provider. But, I know that making friends is such a challenge for her and it was a safe place to start making friends. While Hikarih originally did not want to attend the social skills group, I insisted that she attend at least three groups and then I would let her decide whether she wanted to go again. A compromise. By prompting her to try something out of her comfort zone, Hikarih had some positive experiences. With the help and coaching of the professionals, two actual friends came out of it. They don't see each other that often in face-to-face interaction, but they have maintained regular contact through online social media outlets and through online games. (Hikarih's mom, Hikarih is a young adult with ASD)

There are often groups that connect young adults and teens with ASD with others in the community for social events. Similarly, there are also "meetup" groups that connect people based on a common interest. These could be a helpful way to begin socializing if you are worried about "fitting in."

From Hikarih's story, several recommendations emerged related to meeting people. First, it is important sometimes to push yourself a bit beyond your comfort zone. While Hikarih did not originally want to go to the social event, some positive things came out of it—including two new friends. Limiting the number of times she had to go put Hikarih in control of the situation and made the situation less overwhelming. Setting compromises like this may be helpful for you as well.

In addition to social groups established by mental health professionals, many colleges and university students are interested in learning more about autism spectrum disorders, while socializing at the same time. These programs that focus on facilitating interactions between those with and without ASD can be a great, safe starting point for forming new relationships. Young adults in college communities can organize social events that include young adults on the spectrum. For instance, students at one university joined with students and young adults with ASD through a local ASD-focused organization to have monthly social events (e.g., spring fling dance, game nights, recreational events and scavenger hunts).

> The social events were great for everyone, both on and off of the spectrum. Lots of the participants with ASD mentioned that it was so nice to have a safe social event that was "normal" and like what they saw on television and/or heard about from peers. Having the spring fling dance at the university was great because the young adults with ASD got to see the campus and interact socially with people their own age. It was also nice to mix people with and without autism so not everyone at the event had a diagnosis. While initially, everyone was a little bit nervous and hesitant, within a half hour or so, people started being themselves and having fun. By having these events on campus, it slowly becomes a campus that embraces and appreciates individuals with autism and diversity in general. (Danielle age 20, neuro-typical college student)

Once you have developed some friendships, the next step is to figure out some activities that you and your friends may be interested in doing together. Where you socialize will depend largely on the nature of your friendship, your shared interests, access to transportation and finances. You might prefer getting together with friends in relatively calm and predictable venues (e.g., at home, at the movies, the park), but meetups, safe parties, pubs or clubs can also be popular destinations.

Meetups

Meetup (www.meetup.com) is the world's largest network of groups and group activities that are local to your area and specific to a shared interest. On Meetup, individuals can join an existing group or start their own. The organizers of the group develop a topic and name for the group, which usually indicates the topic or shared interest, for example: *Comic Book Meetup*, *Anime Discovery* and *Coding Group*. The great thing about the groups on Meetup is that you get access to the names and faces of the individuals (along with a short introduction) before ever meeting them face to face. As well, most "meetups" occur in a public area with multiple people and the majority (nearly 90%) are totally free. Of those with an associated fee, the cost is minimal and specific to covering the cost of the activity. The benefits of public, local, specialized and free groups are numerous, and they are an accessible and convenient way for you to meet new people that you have something in common with.

Parties, Pubs and Clubs

I had a Halloween party at my house and felt really unsafe at a few points. It got out of control and I had a bunch of friends there that were close to me that helped out. There were about 40 people at the apartment and I didn't know what to do—I was totally freaked out about it. If you are having a party, it's a good idea to have people there who have complementary strengths. For example, I struggle with assertiveness so having my friend there that is assertive really helped get the situation under control. The buddy system really works. (Aaron, young adult with ASD)

While parties, pubs and clubs are other potential venues for meeting many different new people at one time, they also require a heightened awareness of potential safety issues. When it comes to parties, it is important to start smart—do not select the most crowded establishment or the biggest party of the year, especially if this is your first event. Attending the event with a buddy will likely help you feel more comfortable and ready to engage in new social interactions. Parties and large venues may be overwhelming at times so it is important to understand safety rules, such as underage drinking laws, before you set out for a night on the town.

CONSIDERATIONS ABOUT PARTIES

- Unlike bars or restaurants, parties are less structured, regulated settings and are more likely to have underage drinking, drug use, sexual activities, etc.

- Additionally, because many house/dorm parties will be occurring in residential neighborhoods or apartments with others who are not attending the party, there is potential for law enforcement to be called. Ensuring that you not violating any laws (e.g., underage drinking, etc.) is especially important.

- If you are the host of a party, it is important to limit your guest list to people you know and trusted friends of friends. However, having uninvited guests is a risk you take when having a party. While you can refuse to let people in who are unfamiliar or with whom you are uncomfortable, this can be an awkward and sometimes confrontational situation.

- If a situation escalates or a fight breaks out at your party, you should inform the police immediately.

- If police do get involved, remember to be cooperative and compliant and don't flee the scene, which could result in more consequences. While it is normal to be scared, the best advice is to stay put and cooperate.

- The buddy system is crucial—if you are having or attending a party, it is wise to do so with a trusted friend or family member. Ideally, you and your friend will have skill sets that complement one another.

People with ASD need to remember that things might come across differently to you and people pick up on that. I've had bad experiences at clubs just trusting people. You really have to be aware and realize that you need to be more aware than the average person. Have a plan if something happens. Try to find out the relevant numbers for security/police before you go just in case you need to contact them. If a fight breaks out at a club, you need a plan. Some people drop everything when they get anxious, then they have a meltdown. Going over what you need to do before you go can be very reassuring to the situation. (Aaron, young adult with ASD)

If you have limited social experiences and other skills (money management problems or a poor sense of direction), take it slow in your introduction to bar and party scenarios. It is important to assess your skill set closely to determine if your individual life and social skills are developed enough to manage these situations. In order to consider going out to nightclubs/pubs/parties safely, you should have a relatively strong set of skills already in place (see Tip 1.4).

TIP 1.4 Skills for safely navigating nightclubs

☑ Have a cell phone and know how to use it for identifying public transportation routes, hailing a car service, communicating with your roommates/parents and other party goers about location and safety.

☑ The ability to drive, utilize public transportation and/ or arrange a ride to and from a social event is necessary. Additionally, basic navigational skills are a must for you to get to and from a party safely.

☑ Understand how to use a credit card to "start a tab," how to check bills for accuracy, appropriate tipping etiquette and what to do if your card is lost/stolen.

☑ You should be comfortable monitoring your alcohol intake and regulating your behavior.

Sensitivities and Anxieties

I have to prepare myself for things like noise levels and the amount of people there. If I consider these factors beforehand and prepare for it, I can usually manage. (Molly, young adult with ASD)

The first few times that you go out with friends, particularly to social venues like pubs, bars or clubs, it is wise to go with people you trust or know well. You may even want to scope out a popular club or bar/restaurant with your family prior to going out with your friends. This is a good way to ease anxiety by familiarizing yourself with the setting, and allows you to identify a "safe space" for a sensory break, if needed. As you can imagine, going to a crowded bar, pub or party can be an assault on your sensory system (see Tip 1.5).

TIP 1.5 Potential sensory issues in public venues

☑ Loud music (possible thumping of the bass that is experienced physically).

☑ Loud conversations and yelling.

☑ Dancing.

☑ People invading your personal space.

☑ Strong odors (perfume, cologne, body odors, food and drink smells).

☑ Temperature is often warm in a crowded location.

It's overwhelming because there are lots of people. I remember dances in middle school and high school and being "OMG—what do I do?" The key for me is to have a good time. Have fun with your friends and let the chips fall where they do. Also, I often have so many expectations and will not want to go to a social event in case it will not work out. When I focus on one thing (e.g., "I hope my favorite song comes on" or "I hope I get to dance with a certain person") I can let that ruin my time. (Alex, young adult with ASD)

If you are interested in going to parties and/or bars, try starting out only going for limited periods of time. Perhaps the first few times, go only for 30–60 minutes rather than being there for many hours. Having control over your transportation (e.g., driving yourself, going to a location in which public transportation is accessible, having a family member or friend pick you up, taking a taxi) is a smart idea when planning to limit the amount of time. Also, choosing to go to somewhere more relaxed and quiet or at a non-peak time may help you develop confidence.

You may experience getting fixated on aspects of going out based on your individual anxieties, sensory issues or the need for sameness and repetition. It is best to approach the social event with realistic expectations and recognize when you are getting frustrated or anxious. Knowing your triggers can help you adjust and tap into your regulatory skills or make the decision to leave and remove yourself from an undesirable situation. Remember, the goal is to have a fun and safe time. It is important to prepare for these social events so that you can enjoy a nice time with friends, meet new people and have new positive experiences (see Tip 1.6).

TIP 1.6 **Managing sensory overload**

☑ Be physically prepared—get plenty of rest, eat before going to the venue and stay hydrated.

☑ Wear foam ear plugs to reduce noise—you can still hear and have conversations, but it minimizes sensory overload.

☑ Wear sunglasses in locations with bright lights.

☑ Take a sensory break—at least once every hour or more if you need it; step outside or find a quiet location away from the stimulation.

☑ Limit the amount of time you spend at the social event, especially in your first few outings.

☑ Dress in layers to provide more control over the temperature.

☑ Use positive pressure to calm the nervous system—this can be accomplished by wearing a tight spandex shirt underneath your clothes.

☑ Bring a stress ball or other sensory device that fits in your coat or pants pocket.

Arriving Safely: The Logistics
Transportation
When considering going out with friends, transportation is a key issue. Finding a safe and reliable ride to and from the social event requires advanced planning and is vital to your safety. Always have a back-up plan in place if the original

location changes. You should know how you are getting to and from this new location, particularly if you have been drinking. Having driving alternatives set up in advance (e.g., Uber, Lyft, cab numbers, parents "on call") will ensure you have a safe ride home. Keep in mind the following when arranging transportation:

- If you are driving, make sure your car has adequate gas. Ideally having over a half a tank of gas is recommended as a minimum amount.

- Taking a car that is safe and up to date on service/ maintenance is ideal.

- If you plan to drink at all, you should not drive. The convenience of driving is not worth the risks (e.g., legal, financial, health-related) of driving while under the influence. Do not take a ride from anyone who is drinking or using drugs or alcohol. See Chapter 5 for a more detailed discussion about driving under the influence.

- While taking public transportation is a good option, be sure to have the money you need (i.e., exact change, a pre-purchased pass or a credit card) and that you are very familiar with the schedule and times of service.

- In the case of public transportation, don't go it alone. When it is late or dark outside, you may be putting yourself in a vulnerable position by being in an isolated location after dark. Remember there is safety in numbers.

- Changing locations often requires more money in the form of an additional cover charge, additional parking fees or transportation costs.

Notification

> There were some really shady people at a friend's house once so I decided to text my sister (and a few people) giving them the address just in case something happened. (Aaron, young adult with ASD)

It is always a good idea to let people know where you are so they will be able to locate you in case of an emergency. A family member or friend may need to get in touch with you but might not be able to do so if your battery died or you could not hear the phone ringing because of the noise level in the club. Though uncommon, it is possible that something bad could happen to you that leaves you unable to get home safely or contact your family/friends. You will want to ensure that others know you are safe while out, or if you plan to be late. You may also decide that you are having a great time and want to stay out later than you initially planned. No matter what the reason, keeping relevant friends and family updated about your plans prevents them from worrying about you unnecessarily and is a beneficial safety strategy. Some recommendations about notifications are listed below.

CONSIDERATIONS ABOUT NOTIFYING FRIENDS AND FAMILY WHEN YOU ARE SOCIALIZING

- Be sure to tell your family and friends where you are going and leave an address and phone number of your destination if possible.

- Tell relevant people your best estimate of the time you plan to be home.

- If plans change, as they often do, be sure to update your family and friends (e.g., you decide to stay at a friend's house instead of going home).

- Tell your friends or family who you are going with. It is also a good idea to provide your family/trusted friend with the contact information for your friend in case your cell phone gets lost or stolen, etc. Note: you may also want to install a "find my phone" app on your phone in case you do lose it. Know how to use this feature on another phone to try to locate yours.

- Have a timeline regarding when you plan to leave and stick to it as much as possible. Again, update necessary friends/family members if you plan to deviate significantly from your original time.

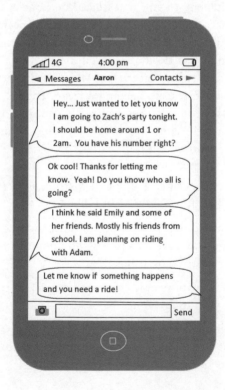

Communication

Due to the unpredictable nature of socializing and the lurking safety issues that accompany it, it is important that you stay connected with people. Staying in touch with your family and friends is a great way to minimize your anxiety while out and about. Technology has given us the opportunity to be in nearly constant contact via phone, text and email. Also, the number of apps that can be downloaded to your phone to assist with safety is astounding—be sure to take advantage and explore some apps that may help you and your family. When you go out, be sure that you have your phone with you and that it is fully charged. You may also want to keep an emergency phone charger handy (i.e., a charger that works rapidly without electricity). Of course a phone is not very helpful if you are not proficient at using it or do not have the necessary numbers or apps in your phone. If you decide to leave early or change locations, or there is an emergency, having access to your phone is both necessary and convenient. The following suggestions highlight safety precautions related to staying connected while socializing:

- **Use your smartphone to socialize smart**—load your phone up with apps and phone numbers that can be of assistance in a different scenarios (e.g., AAA, local emergency numbers, cab companies, towing, Uber, Lyft, numbers of family and friends).

- **Charge it**—make sure you phone is charged before you leave and ideally bring your charger (or purchase an emergency charger) just in case.

- **Be sure to close all of your unnecessary applications** that are open on your phone because they can quickly drain your battery.

- **Have money or a credit card in case of emergency** (i.e., in case you need a ride home because your driver seems to be drinking too much).

- **Expect problems**—in certain locations (i.e., the bar, restaurant or party) there may not be good reception for your phone or access to the internet. You also may have difficulty hearing someone you are talking to in a noisy and crowded place.

- **Avoid isolated locations** that can make you vulnerable.

Preparation for going out will help you understand logistics about the social event before you go. Planning can be complex and challenging but will ensure you have a fun, safe time once you are at the event. (See Social Script 1.1, which is a conversation between two friends as they discuss logistics about a party they are attending together that evening.)

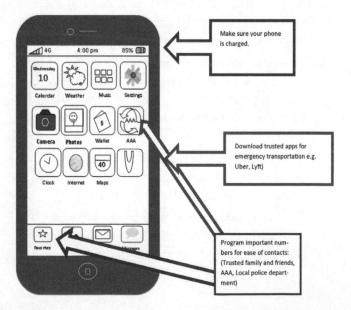

42

**SOCIAL SCRIPT 1.1 PLANNING AND DISCUSSING
A SOCIAL EVENT WITH A FRIEND**

Christopher: "So Kate, you mentioned that there is a party at Layne's house. Do you know any other details about the party? I don't even know where she lives."

Kate: "Layne lives in the apartments near the mall. I think it is only going to be a few people since her place is small. We should plan how to get there—do you want to drive or should I pick you up?"

Christopher: "I can drive since I don't drink—what time does it start?"

Kate: "She said anytime after 8:00, but I was thinking of going around 10:00."

Christopher: "What else should I know about the party? I have not been to very many parties, so I don't know what to expect—should I bring something?"

As you can see in the social script above, friends go through a natural negotiation about transportation and communication about an event. They also tend to compare other specifics like clothing choices for the party and what to bring. Details are an important part of socializing and there are certain things you need to know before you go (see Tip 1.7).

TIP 1.7 **Things to know before you go**

☑ Get relevant details of the event if possible (e.g., start time, location, dress code).

☑ Time for arriving/leaving.

☑ Who will be there.

☑ What activities will be happening.

☑ An emergency contact in case things go wrong (e.g., friends, parents).

Peer Victimization and Bullying

While I have experienced some explicit bullying when I was younger, more recently, I mainly feel misunderstood by others. I have trouble explaining my challenges and preferences to others without disclosing my diagnosis—making me seem even more "different"). I do not like to be touched but it is very hard to tell people that because I worry that they may think I am weird or being impolite. For instance, a guy at work always slapped me on the back unannounced and it felt like "razor blades" to me. I told my supervisor, but he did not really seem to understand or support my needs—they think it is an excuse. Overall, I want to fit in but I need help doing so. Also, when girls flirt they are "touchy," which is a challenge because of my sensitivity to touch. If you don't want attention from girls, they assume you are "gay" or call you names. Again, I just feel misunderstood. (Patrick, young adult with ASD)

In this neuro-typical world of mixed messages and unwritten social rules, it can be difficult for many to interpret the actions and intentions of others, illustrated by the quote below:

> It is unclear to me if people are joking or not. Some people insult one another as part of their friendship. A lot of people treat their friends rude and it is hard to tell if there is actual bullying going on or if they are messing around. (Neal, young adult with ASD)

Joking around is a great way to interact with your peers. However, innocent jokes and insults can quickly transform into harsher attacks directly aimed at one another. Comments that seem insulting can be interpreted as funny or even a sign of friendship when said in a lighthearted way or if the person making them is a friend. However, some actions are undeniably hurtful and mean. Bullying is defined as a relational problem (a relationship between two people or a group of people that is not working well interpersonally) that includes repetitive hostile interactions (e.g., physical, verbal and emotional) that are linked to a power differential within the relationship.[2] People who are bullied often experience negative effects including depression, low self-esteem, psychosomatic symptoms (e.g., headaches and stomach aches, etc.) and impaired academic and occupational achievement.[3] One of the best things about individuals with ASD like you is that you often take everyone at face value and are trusting of other people; however, because individuals with ASD can be so trusting, they can often be victimized by others in a variety of ways, including financially, sexually, legally, etc.

---

2 Pepler and Craig (2000)
3 Grills and Ollendick (2002)

The biggest concern I see is that the individuals with ASD that I work with don't know when it is happening. They'll say, "Yes, I have a friend," but when we observe the interaction we realize they are not a friend. A lot of our clients are working and more often than not there are coworkers picking on them. Job coaches are not very familiar with assisting employees with ASD. I talk to them about being a "social spy." I work with them (the job coach) to recognize when someone is being picked on. Looking to read the verbal and non-verbal signs that someone is/is not their friend or picking on them. (Beth Thompson, Milestones Autism Resources, social worker with specialization in young adults with ASD)

Unfortunately, bullying and victimization come in many shapes and sizes and occur in many different locations. Whether the bullying occurs in the community, the workplace or the school, it is helpful to be aware of the signs and have strategies in place to address bullying when/if it occurs to you or someone you know. You could be a target of bullying for potentially violating a social norm (i.e., talking too much about a certain topic or being too rule bound) or because you have difficulty reading the social cues or behaviors that might indicate someone is taking advantage of you. A recent study reported that nearly 50 percent of adolescents with ASD are victims of bullying,[4] approximately two times as many as the general population. This is definitely a safety concern and something that requires you to learn some proactive prevention strategies.

I'm an extremely trusting person and a lot of times people pick up on this, just like when you are kids. A good kid will believe or do anything you say and people exploit that.

---

4   Sterzing *et al.* (2012)

> It happens in the workplace as well. Its not name calling or physical bullying but more exploitation. Working security, someone might ask me to watch something and they go off and do what they want knowing that I have to stay there and watch it. (Aaron, young adult with ASD)

While some bullying is more extreme and explicit, other forms of bullying can be more indirect, but still upsetting (i.e., feeling left out, being discriminated against or feeling misunderstood) and can have a negative impact on your self-esteem.

> I have been both bullied and ignored. For me, being ignored was much worse. It's heart-breaking to have nobody who thinks about you or wants to talk to you. Bullying was easier because I am good at coming up with withering responses. (Molly, young adult with ASD)

While prevention is ideal, due to the nature of bullying, it can be difficult to systematically prevent it from happening. The cause of the bullying lies *within the bully*—it is never your fault if bullying or victimization does occur—but it is important to know how to deal with bullies in case you encounter these unfortunate situations (see Tips 1.8 and 1.9).

TIP 1.8 Avoiding bullies

☑ **Educate yourself**—be aware that you may be more vulnerable to bullying because of a tendency to be naïve and socially vulnerable.

☑ **Try to avoid being in vulnerable or unfamiliar situations** with people you don't know.

☑ **There is safety in numbers**—having trusted friends/family around can help support you and help you determine if someone is a positive person in your life.

☑ **Familiarize yourself with appropriate contacts** related to bullying/victimization issues at school or the workplace (i.e., human resources, dean of students, police, etc.) to talk to if bullying should occur, and know ways to respond to bullying as outlined below. There are several strategies that can be employed to address bullying if it happens to you.

Our daughter has her first group of friends in her life. We've been burned in the past by a couple of people who seemed to befriend her and turned out to be using her. My husband and I were initially so grateful to these people—before we knew what their motives were—that we went out of our way to treat them as very special to us. One of these people was a boyfriend of three years that we treated like family—taking him out to dinner with us, giving him nice gifts for holidays and birthdays. We found out that he had been stealing from our daughter's bank account, but he would not admit to it. We try to teach our daughter how to act as a friend and how to identify when she is being taken advantage of. (Priscilla, mother of young adult with ASD)

TIP 1.9 Warning signs that someone might not be good friend for you

Unfortunately, sometimes people who seem kind and friendly are just using you. Be skeptical of people who:

☑ pressure others to do things that are wrong or illegal

☑ want money or access to personal accounts

☑ seem too good to be true (i.e., the most popular guy in the fraternity wants to be your friend unexpectedly after ignoring you or mistreating you for months)

☑ mistreat or insult others

☑ are physically or verbally abusive (you should get help from families and professionals if this happens)

☑ do not follow through with promises or obligations.

So often the bullies operate quietly and then when the victim gets angry and frustrated it is often the victim that gets punished unfairly. It's the good old—"second punch always gets seen first." The more malicious bullies whisper or know how to go "under the radar" while our kids tolerate it for a certain amount of time then "get caught" standing up for themselves. (Anne, parent of young adult with ASD)

Though it is helpful to know the warning signs and strategies to avoid bullying, figuring out what to do when bullying does occur is just as crucial. While the majority of bullying situations need to be handled on a case-by-case basis, for more traditional forms of bullying like name-calling, snide remarks and physical threats, there are some general guidelines that can be helpful to you. First, try not to react or show the individual(s) that you are upset. Oftentimes, bullies get their feelings/perceptions of power and control from the your reaction. If you become agitated, frustrated or sad, the intimidator feels control over you. While it is totally understandable to be upset and want to express your frustration, try to stay calm, walk away or call for help right away if you feel physically threatened. You should always tell someone about the bullying. Suffering alone does not help you, nor does it address the bully's behavior.

Get help! Recruit friends or even bystanders to assist when necessary. It is also important to report incidents to the proper authorities to maintain your safety and to help prevent future instances of bullying. While the first person you contact may not be helpful, don't give up or be discouraged. If little or nothing is done to address your concerns initially, you should report the incident to the next highest person in authority until the issue is addressed sufficiently. If the bullying or harassment becomes very serious and threatening, you may need to contact the police or other security personnel immediately. Know your rights! Bullying is a form of harassment and can have significant legal consequences if it is not addressed.

> My advice for an individual who is experiencing bullying is to explicitly tell the bully to stop the bullying behavior. I also suggest that they tell the teacher or professor but not more than once. The next step should be taking the complaint to their supervisor and so on until someone does something about it. I say, scare the system into doing what you need them to do. (Neal, young adult with ASD)

If possible, educate your school, place of work and community about bullying issues. Peer or bystander intervention is a critical part of stopping the cycle of bullying and intimidation. Studies have shown that bullying is significantly reduced when peers intervene;[5] however, because you may lack social connections, you can be more at risk. If an incident of bullying does occur, rather than ignore it, it can be helpful for you to process what happened, emphasizing things that were handled well and things that need improvement if a similar scenario arises again. When Patrick, a young adult with ASD, has a challenging social interaction, he and his family (mom, dad and sister) do a "social autopsy" of the situation. For example, when Patrick had an altercation with a coworker who accused him of getting him in trouble with a supervisor, the family discussed some possible reasons the individual accused him, how he managed the confrontation and how he could improve his response in the future.

> Bullying is the biggest issue I see in student support services at the university despite the fact that we have a well-established bullying protocol. I also think it is important for students and parents to know their rights; once it is recognized as harassment, it is considered a legal issue (which gives the victim enhanced rights) and could result in the bully being removed from the school or workplace. My son was being bullied for several weeks in class and his professor did very little to address it. However, I have really pushed my son to be his own self-advocate—so in this instance, he was the one who went to the dean of students and reported it. (Anne, mother of young adult with ASD)

---

5   Polanin, Espelage and Piggot (2012)

It is easy to let bullying affect your self-esteem and mental health. If you are feeling upset or depressed about a bullying situation, it is very important to tell your friends, family or mental health professional what is going on so they can provide you with support and guidance. You are not alone. There are many hotlines, websites and support groups.[6]

It can be tempting just to go along with a supervisor who seems to minimize a situation involving bullying and intimidation, but it is important to document these types of incidents. Without intervention and documentation, things could get much worse. Also, by documenting what happened you have more power in case of another incident. Reporting is a way to transfer power from the bully to victim. If you are having trouble knowing what to do or say, especially if you are getting resistance about reporting it—get help from a friend, family member or other coworker that you trust.

Summary

Socializing safely has a multitude of benefits. Even though it can be stressful for you to navigate the social world, the benefits can truly outweigh the challenges. While meeting people can be challenging, there are many ways (both in person and online) you can meet people with similar interests to enhance your social network.

While socializing is meant to be fun, failure to take precautions can lead you into unsafe territory. Meeting people through appropriate channels, preparing yourself for sensory

---

6   www.stopbullying.gov and a cyberbullying hotline: 1-800-420-1479;
    Bullying UK (UK only) www.bullying.co.uk (0808-800-2222);
    Kids Helpline (Australia only) www.kidshelp.com.au (1800-55-180)
    and bullyingnoway.gov.au; Kids Help Phone (Canada only) www.
    kidshelpphone.ca (800-668-6868) and www.bullyingcanada.ca

challenges, making responsible transportation decisions, notifying family and friends about your plans, knowing who to trust, understanding the norms associated with pubs/clubs/ parties and knowing how to manage bullying can make a significantly positive difference. Be yourself, have fun and be safe—a new friend or engaging life experience awaits!

SOCIAL SCRIPT 1.2 HOW TO REPORT BULLYING

Reporting bullying can be awkward, embarrassing and hard to do. The following example is one way to begin the conversation with a supervisor when reporting a bullying situation at work. While the wording may differ slightly, you can modify the script for similar situations (e.g., school, in social settings, etc.).

Kenny: "I am not really sure how to say this, but I wanted to let you know that my coworker, Mickey, has been giving me a hard time—making fun of me, intimidating me physically. I am not sure what to do."

Matt: "Well, can you tell me what happened? I can't imagine Mickey would do something like that—are you sure you didn't just misunderstand—sometimes you get confused about 'people stuff.'"

Kenny: "I am not confused. He threatened to beat the crap out of me if I looked at his girlfriend again. I don't like his girlfriend—I don't even know her. Mickey also called me some rude names and threw some of my things across the room."

Matt: "Well, OK, but I don't want to report this—too much paperwork. Besides, I don't want to get him in trouble—he's a good worker."

> **Kenny:** "I remember from my job orientation—you are supposed to report situations like this. If you don't want to report it, I can tell someone else who will."

References

Grills, A. E. and Ollendick, T. H. (2002) 'Peer victimization, global self-worth, and anxiety in middle school children.' *Journal of Clinical Child and Adolescent Psychology 31,* 1, 59–68.

Pepler, D. J. and Craig, W. (2000) *Making a Difference in Bullying.* LaMarsh Report. Toronto, ON: LaMarsh Centre for Research on Violence and Conflict Resolution, York University.

Polanin, J. R., Espelage, D. L. and Pigott, T. D. (2012) 'A meta-analysis of school-based bullying prevention programs' effects on bystander intervention behavior.' *School Psychology Review 41,* 1, 47–65.

Rigler, M., Rutherford, A. and Quinn, E. (2015) *Developing Identity, Strengths, and Self-perception for Young Adults with Autism Spectrum Disorder: The BASICS College Curriculum.* London: Jessica Kingsley Publishers.

Sterzing, P. R., Shattuck, P. T., Narendorf, S. C., Wagner, M. and Cooper, B. P. (2012) 'Bullying involvement and autism spectrum disorders: Prevalence and correlates of bullying involvement among adolescents with an autism spectrum disorder.' *Archives of Pediatrics and Adolescent Medicine 166,* 11, 1058–1064.

Chapter 2

"Friend Me"

Safe and Healthy Relationships

TOP SAFETY CONCERNS

★ Building (and defining) relationships.

★ Dating.

★ Vulnerability and trust.

★ Hurt feelings and managing expectations.

★ Maintaining boundaries—harassment and stalking.

I have always wanted friends, real friends, people that wanted to be around me because they liked me. Not because my parents were having a party with their friends, not because my family was there, but because people really want to be around me. I finally have that and couldn't be happier. (SG, young adult with ASD)

Forming relationships can be difficult for anyone, but developing and navigating relationships can be especially difficult if you are on the spectrum. The subtle and nuanced non-verbal communication between two people is almost a foreign language in and of itself. Why, for example, would a young boy ignore or poke fun of a girl if he likes her? For that matter, if someone likes you, why would he or she wait three days to text or call you?

The actions of others are often muddied by their beliefs about the right way to approach a situation, making deciphering them more laborious. While most people would benefit from a more direct and transparent discussion about their feelings for and towards one another, the reality is that most conversations around romance and relationships are neither clear nor direct. People like to protect themselves (e.g., their feelings, well-being, image, etc.) and avoid hurting others. When communication around relationships is coded in these socially or media-driven messages, it can lead to misunderstandings or missed cues, which contribute to mixed messages about friendships, romance and relationships in general.

> I always thought I had to follow some type of equation. For example, I had to call her at a certain point or we had to see each other a certain number of times to get to the next level. But that doesn't always have to happen. You just need to find a person who has the same mindset as you. When you're with the right person, everything will fall into place and there won't be so many games or rules to follow. (Dave, young adult with ASD)

Mass media often contributes to our beliefs about the "rules" or "expectations" of dating. Let's go back to the longstanding belief that you should wait three days after a date before contacting the person, so as not to seem overly interested or eager. Magazine articles and online dating advice add to this confusion. A recent online article in *Glamour* magazine titled "The delicate politics of dating and Instagram" confirms the difficulties of dating in a world dominated by social media. The article discusses the lack of formal etiquette for social media (see our recommendations in Chapter 4) and how people have varying views on acceptable social media behavior. The *Glamour* article offers guidance around social media use while dating, including such rules as "Don't post photos of each other on Instagram until you are officially dating," and "Don't Instagram your food on a date." One thing is very clear in this social-media-driven world: the ability to navigate these delicate items can have major consequences on relationships. Another snapshot of advice, this time from *Cosmopolitan* online magazine, suggests to women: "DO let him know you have other offers." This is similar to the unspoken, "game playing," cat-and-mouse advice so prevalent in society that has an underlying message: *play hard to get.* The logic behind this advice is that men enjoy the chase and want things that they might not be able to have. The magazine suggests that, "Letting a guy know he has competition is never a bad thing. You can drop hints that you won't be around forever by saying something like: 'What do you see this as?' I ask because I have guys asking me out and I'm not sure what to tell them."[1] They suggest that this method of communication, "lets him know that you are in-demand and can easily be snapped up if he doesn't get serious soon." These articles and the advice within them can be very difficult to understand. What these articles are really suggesting is that when people are overly aggressive and commit to a relationship too quickly, it can scare the other person and push him or her away. While we are not suggesting that you lie to the person you are in a new relationship with, we are suggesting that you take things slowly and do not express a desire for exclusivity too early. Given the multilayered and coded behavior of individuals, it

---

1   Hussey (2015)

is a wonder we ever figure out relationships, much less how to define them!

Defining Relationships

You might also struggle with characterizing and defining relationships. Not understanding where you are in a relationship can lead to safety issues. You might assume someone is your girl/boyfriend and later be accused of stalking—or you might assume you are just friends only to find yourself on the receiving end of attempt for a physical encounter. Understanding the transition from acquaintance to friendship, to dating and, finally, entering into a committed romantic relationship, is important to avoid potential safety issues, but the transition can be difficult. This chapter will help you navigate and better understand the tumultuous waters of relationship building. As you enter into adulthood, you will experience multiple types of relationships with a myriad of people. For most, the people who enter your life will teach you something about the world, about others and about yourself, whether good or bad. Beginning and ending relationships helps us grow and learn. At the end of the day, relationships are all about communication and ensuring that both people are on the same page and that the relationship is healthy and balanced for everyone!

The Beginning: "An Acquaintance"

Every relationship has a beginning. This often results in two people meeting and/or finding some common ground, like enjoying an interest, hobby, shared major at school or specialty at work. At this point, when you don't know another person well, but decide that you would like to know him or her better, you can define the person as an acquaintance. Sometimes we meet an acquaintance through a friend or we meet a new person on our own. If you are interested in expanding your social network, starting with friends of friends and developing more acquaintances is a good start. You might find that you really enjoy an acquaintance and may seek out that person for more interaction or to share a meal or activity. The goal of spending more time together is to determine if you like the person enough to invest in a friendship or something more (i.e., romantic relationship, business partner, etc.).

Once people spend time together more often, they usually either move to a friendship status or remain acquaintances and the relationship stalls with neither party investing the time to maintain or build it. Sometimes people meet and develop their initial friendship online and then work towards a face-to-face relationship. If you are worried about interacting in person, or want to "test the waters" a bit before investing in a face-to-face meeting, you can often test out an acquaintance relationship via online/social networking, exchanging Twitter handles or cell phone numbers for texting. This can give people a better idea about one another's interests, activities and personality. From acquaintance, relationships often stall (this is normal!) with one (or more than one) party not being interested in getting to know the person more or developing the friendship or any other relationship. Alternatively, people may decide that they would like to begin a friendship with this person. Regardless of how you find your relationships developing, many acquaintances will remain just that—people you know and do not dislike, but who never develop into friends (see the figure "Acquaintance options").

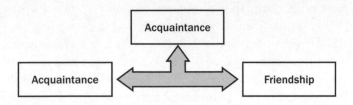

Acquaintance options

The other unfortunate reality in the development of the acquaintance–friend transition is that the feelings may not always be mutual. While one person may decide that he really likes a new acquaintance and wants to develop the relationship into a friendship, the other person may not feel the same way. People almost never explicitly state that they are not interested in becoming friends, which could be considered rude, but instead will not return calls or texts, will repeatedly not be able to get together, etc. If someone fails to show signs of wishing to develop the relationship, or shows signs of not wishing to develop it, it is important that you respect their decision. If you continue to pursue an acquaintance who is giving off signs (see Tip 2.1) of disinterest in developing a friendship, it could actually be interpreted as stalking behavior, which will be discussed later in this chapter.

TIP 2.1 **Signs that someone may not want to develop a relationship**

☑ Not returning phone calls or not picking up when you call.

☑ Not initiating contact.

☑ Turning down offers to get together.

☑ Not responding to texts.

☑ Turning away or trying to hide or act busy when you approach them.

☑ Not engaging in conversations when you attempt to initiate them.

"Friend" Me...

Facebook coined the now everyday saying, "friend me." The act of "friending" is a very social activity that connects people in a virtual environment. By "friending" people, you gain access to their social world and get a glimpse into their likes/dislikes and everyday activities. There are benefits and drawbacks that come along with this type of interaction—for more information on this topic, see Chapter 4. With the popularity of Facebook, the interpretation of friendship has become even more confusing. Now, we more loosely refer to people as our friends, even if we don't know very much about them at all. For example, it is very common for teens and young adults to have over 500 friends on Facebook; logistically, it is nearly *impossible* to initiate, maintain and foster 500 true friendships. Needless to say, the term "friend" in this context is very confusing.

Defining Friendship

So what is an actual friend? A friend is defined as, "one attached to another by affection or esteem," while an acquaintance is defined as, "someone who is known but who is not a close friend."[2] True friends are close to one another; they know details about each other's lives, like their personal interests and even family life. Friends also enjoy shared activities and engage in these at regular intervals.

Friendships come in different levels of intensity, which are often related to the duration of the friendship. It is important to identify where a particular friendship is positioned on the friendship level (see the figure "Friendship levels"), in order to understand what is expected within the relationship. An *everyday friend* is someone with whom you interact frequently due to specific circumstances (e.g., you share a class, are in the same grade, work together daily), but in the absence of the shared structure, the friendship would fail to thrive. These are people you know well, but do not necessarily translate into life-long friends. If you and the everyday friend started meeting outside of the structured activity and shared a lot in common, the friendship might transition to a *developed friendship,* one that is supported and grows as a result of the motivation to see each other outside of the structure that formed the everyday friendship. Finally, people can consider themselves very lucky to have a few life-long friends. A *life-long friendship* is supported by maintenance, shared activities and shared life experiences. Individuals in these relationships are highly invested in the friendship and share a strong bond, trust and mutual respect for one another that transcends time and proximity.

---

2   The Merriam-Webster online dictionary

Everyday friendships	Developed friendship	Life-long friend
		Friendship supported by years of maintenance and shared activities. Friendship has usually crossed many moments (e.g., college, marriage, breakups, children, jobs).
	Friendship supported by extra effort to see the individual outside of normal everyday activities.	People usually know a great deal about one another and have a high level of trust between them.
Friendship supported by mutual activities but not sustained outside of structured/planned activities (e.g., a school mate, dorm mate, work friend, someone you see only at club meetings).	Shared interest in other activities, general feelings of support by interacting with the person, system of trust, overall happiness and joy from exchange.	Shared history and bank of memories that involve each other. Does not require daily contact to feel supported. Lifetime investment in each other.
Friendship would fail to thrive outside of present activities.	Friendship requires maintenance to sustain, but highly motivated to invest in friendship.	Friendship doesn't require daily maintenance and can be called upon whenever needed. People considered to be like family.

Friendship levels

Dating

> My definition of dating—when two people are interested in one another and complement each other. For example, for me, I would need someone very social. You need to be attracted to one another but bring out the best in one another. (Alex, young adult with ASD)

Dating is the process of getting to know someone who might be a romantic interest. You might date so that you can enjoy activities with another person you are attracted to in some way or to enjoy a sexual relationship with a committed partner. You might also choose to date as part of a larger goal to find a spouse or life partner. The goals for dating are important, and both parties should be aware of the other's goals before starting to date to avoid any miscommunication and hurt feelings (see the figure "Goals of dating"). For example, you might become disillusioned if you were dating with the goal of getting married, only to find out that the other person was primarily interested in a casual sexual relationship (see Social Script 2.1). Another important part of defining a dating relationship is to know whether or not each person is dating the other person *exclusively*. Being in an exclusive relationship suggests that both parties agree not to date other people. This exclusivity implies a level of commitment to one another that goes beyond that of casual dating and needs to be discussed by both parties when the time is right (i.e., after several dates and the relationship is going well). If you do not wish to date exclusively you could keep things casual and date other people. When dating other people you should make sure that both parties understand this. Also, when dating others it is considered poor form to ask about the other person's relationships.

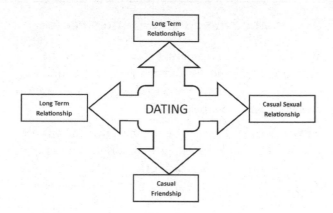

Goals of dating

TIP 2.2 **Signs in a relationship that suggest you are ready to have the "Are we exclusive?" talk**

☑ When you are happy and excited about the relationship, and the person makes you feel good about yourself.

☑ When you feel ready to commit and you suspect the other person feels the same based on things they say or do (i.e., telling you he or she is happy in the relationship, initiating affection with you, planning future dates).

☑ When there is regular (i.e., daily to every other day), two-way communication via phone or text.

☑ When you are making future plans (several weeks to one month in advance).

☑ Before having a sexual relationship with the person.

SOCIAL SCRIPT 2.1 DATING OTHER PEOPLE

When you first begin dating someone, he or she may be dating other people. To begin a conversation about whether you are dating other people, you can use the conversation starter below.

"(Insert name), I'm really enjoying our time together but just want to keep things casual right now. I hope we can continue to see each other, I'm just in a place where I'm not quite ready to get super serious with someone."

What is our "Status?"

Facebook heightened the use of the term *status* (*pertaining to relationships*) and made it a part of everyday language. Your *status* refers to how to define your current state of a relationship (e.g., single, married, engaged, boyfriend/girlfriend, dating). Thanks to Facebook, we also have the status category "It's complicated"—suggesting that the relationship may be in transition (e.g., new, dissolving, dating but not in a committed relationship, not interested in looking for a relationship at the moment despite being single). Anyone who has ever been in a relationship knows that at some point nearly *all* relationships are complicated. This is especially true when the relationship transitions from one phase to another. However, it is important to consider the rationale and consequences related to posting about a private romantic relationship in a public forum. Some people update and change their relationship status as a means of garnering attention or interest about their personal life from others. Someone who changes his or her relationship status and/or romantic partners frequently may not be a stable choice, as it suggests that the individual may not be ready to enter a committed relationship or may have difficulty preserving privacy in a relationship. Also, beware of posting your own relationship status updates frequently. No one should update a relationship status without the consent of the other person. Announcing via social media that you are in a relationship too early can end a relationship before it begins. Remember, the healthiest relationships are those built on communication, honesty, transparency and privacy.

Boyfriend/Girlfriend/Partner

> I would say you are not someone's boyfriend unless you both explicitly state that you are romantically involved. You can have close relationships with people that do not have to be romantic. (Jeremy, young adult with ASD)

When couples decide to date exclusively, they often refer to one another as their boyfriend, girlfriend or partner. This signals to others that the person is in a committed relationship and not available to date others (see Social Script 2.2). This level of commitment requires some negotiation and understanding around the responsibilities and expectations of one another and of the relationship. To avoid hurt feelings and miscommunication, and to ensure that both parties feel safe and secure in the relationship, a minimum number of topics should be addressed (see Tip 2.3). Each of these topics will be addressed at various times and not all at once—*that might be a bit overwhelming!* Remember, relationships are a constant negotiation—especially in the beginning.

**SOCIAL SCRIPT 2.2 EXCLUSIVELY
DATING EACH OTHER**

After dating someone for a period of time, you determine that you would prefer to date only this person and would like the same consideration in return.

"(Insert name) we've been dating now for (insert time period) and I think it is going very well. I am not interested in dating other people and I'd like to see where this goes. Would you be open to being in an exclusive relationship?"

Relationships require frequent communication and a shared vision for the future. It is important to understand where you are in a relationship. When transitioning between relationship levels, you must be willing to commit to actively learning about a person, setting ground rules and respecting the person as an individual. Understanding one another's intentions is critically important. Given the difficulty with deciphering subtle social cues, it takes heightened vigilance to ensure that the other person is moving in an equal fashion and at an equal pace (see the figure "Relationship support structure"). Finding a trusted friend, relative, peer mentor or life coach can help you with getting accurate and honest feedback on relationship issues.[3]

---

3   Advice from The MOSAIC program at the University of Tennessee, Chattanooga

TIP 2.3 Topics for committed relationships

Money

☑ Who will pay for dates?

☑ How will expenses be shared?

Sex

☑ Will you be in a sexual relationship?

☑ What are the boundaries of a sexual relationship?

☑ What is your comfort level?

☑ What are your expectations?

☑ How often will you engage in sex?

☑ What form of protection will you use?

☑ What about sexual preferences/interests?

☑ Will you get tested for sexually transmitted infections/ diseases (STI/STDs) before engaging in sex?

Time

☑ How much time will you spend together?

☑ On dates?

☑ Hanging out?

☑ On the phone?

☑ What are the expectations for returning texts/phone calls or answering emails?

Long-term expectations

☑ What are each party's goals?

☑ Is marriage a long-term goal?

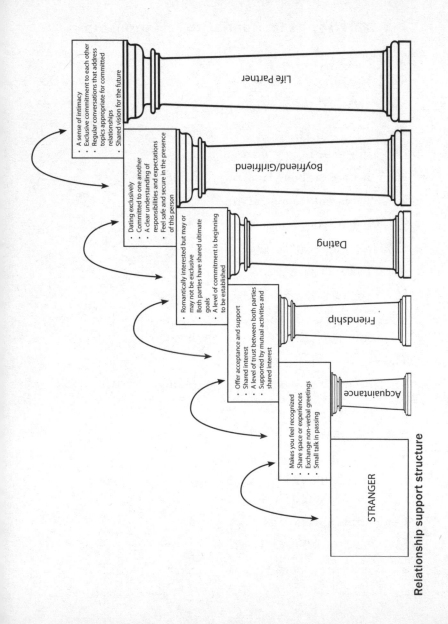

Relationship support structure

Life Partner
- A sense of intimacy
- Exclusive commitment to each other
- Regular conversations that address topics appropriate for committed relationships
- Shared vision for the future

Boyfriend/Girlfriend
- Dating exclusively
- Committed to one another
- A clear understanding of responsibilities and expectations
- Feel safe and secure in the presence of this person

Dating
- Romantically interested but may or may not be exclusive
- Both parties have shared ultimate goals
- A level of commitment is beginning to be established

Friendship
- Offer acceptance and support
- Shared interest
- A level of trust between both parties
- Supported by mutual activities and shared interest

Acquaintance
- Makes you feel recognized
- Share space or experiences
- Exchange non-verbal greetings
- Small talk in passing

STRANGER

Ending a Relationship

> It can be very hurtful. Only time made it better—it's like
> a death of someone. (Aaron, young adult with ASD)

The decision to end a relationship is almost never an easy decision. It may be that your feelings have changed and that you or your significant other no longer wishes to maintain the current relationship status. Sometimes circumstances beyond everyone's control might contribute to the end of a relationship (e.g., moving, going off to school, relocating for work, etc.). Regardless of the reason for the breakup, all breakups result in emotions ranging from relief to sadness, frustration to anger. It is important to understand and accept that emotional highs and lows will occur for a period of time after a breakup and that both parties allow time to grieve the relationship and rebuild their emotional strength.

While most people spend a great deal of time negotiating the beginning of a relationship and the respective boundaries of forming their relationship, they fail to spend an equal amount of time negotiating the end of the relationship. Ending a relationship and maintaining boundaries once the romantic relationship ends are very important. Whether you negotiate a new relationship (e.g., a friendship or an acquaintanceship) or determine that a future relationship with the person is unnecessary or unwanted, both parties must agree on the boundaries and must respect these boundaries. There are very real emotional and legal implications to overstepping these boundaries that can lead to hurt feelings, legal action and even arrest (see the section about stalking on later in this chapter).

Breaking up is rarely a 50/50 decision—usually someone is more upset or hurt, which can make it difficult to make good, clear-headed decisions. It is important that you (and your significant other) utilize all of your supports and coping skills when going through a breakup. Supports may include an existing mental health professional, family members, friends or a support group. Although it can feel embarrassing and humiliating, being on the receiving end of a relationship breakup is something that the majority of people—friends, parents and family members—have experienced. Taking time after a breakup to heal and to surround oneself with a supportive group of friends and family is a necessary part of the grieving process.

As stated in the above quote by Aaron, a breakup can feel like a death and it is important to take time to go through the grieving process. It is also important to remember that good relationships are built on trust and respect, and that people who once had very strong feelings for one another should try to maintain the same level of respect for one another during a breakup. Even if the other party was not respectful to the relationship (e.g., cheating, lying, abuse) it is important to maintain your respectful behavior. Also, staying calm, clear-headed and respectful is a good safety strategy—emotions run high during breakups and you want to avoid making emotional or impulsive decisions that could lead to trouble or trigger unsafe/unkind behavior from you or the other party. Finally, being respectful and mature says a lot about you as an individual and it is a sign of strong character during a breakup.

Harassment

Harassment occurs when one party has contact with another that is unwanted. This can occur via phone, in person, through email or through social media. You might, as a result of ASD traits, truly lack the ability to read the social cues of another person that does not wish to be contacted, but it is essential to try and recognize this. As mentioned before, this is a major safety concern. You don't want to find yourself in legal trouble as a result of misinterpreting a relationship. Tip 2.4 spells out some signs that will help you recognize when another person does not desire contact with you.

TIP 2.4 **Signs that an individual does not desire contact**

☑ Failure to make eye contact.

☑ Not returning phone calls.

☑ Not initiating contact.

☑ Turning down offers to get together.

☑ Not answering phone.

☑ Not returning texts.

☑ Giving non-specific responses to detailed questions.

Further complicating the equation is the reality that others might not understand that you have ASD or that you struggle with the non-verbal and other non-direct social cues. The recipient of your attention may find repetitive attention aggravating or creepy or view the behavior as harassment. Unwanted attention can be very frightening to an individual. Given this, it is essential that you closely monitor your behavior and exchanges with potential friends or romantic interests. Tip 2.5 helps you determine how much communication is too much so you can safely navigate communication with others.

TIP 2.5 **How much communication is too much**

A good rule of thumb is the equal communication 1 = 1 rule. For every text, phone call, email or social media message you send the other person should respond in kind. While not always a sure gauge of interest, most people will stop communicating with someone in whom they have no interest.

If the communication desires of the other party are unknown, *ask* them (see Social Script 2.3). By asking if attention and communication is unwanted, you will be absolutely sure where you stand and can avoid claims of harassment. The consequences for harassment range from alienating the object of your attention to legal interventions (protective order/arrest). It is really important, therefore, to ensure that all attention is welcome (see Tip 2.6).

TIP 2.6 **The 24-hour rule**

When one person expects communication responses instantly, or in a short period of time, it can put a lot of stress on a relationship, especially a new one. Allow the individual 24 hours to respond before reaching out again.

Communication met with silence usually indicates that the person no longer wishes to stay in touch. It is perfectly acceptable to confirm the person's feelings or intentions with a simple question: Am I bothering you? (See Social Script 2.3.)

SOCIAL SCRIPT 2.3 AM I BOTHERING YOU?

If you are concerned that you are potentially communicating too much, you might say to the other person:

"I noticed you are not responding to my (phone calls, emails, texts) and I want to respect your wishes. If you don't wish to communicate, please let me know and I won't contact you again; if you've just been busy it would be helpful to know that as well. Thank you, (name)"

Stalking

Stalking is defined as a pattern of repeated and unwanted attention, harassment, contact or any other course of conduct directed at a specific person that would cause a reasonable person to feel fear.[4] Unfortunately, you may not be attuned to the social cues that show a person is not interested. You could find yourself in a situation where you are considered a stalker even when you believe a friendship or romance has been developed with a person.

Stalking can include the following behaviors

- Repeated, unwanted, intrusive and frightening communications from the perpetrator by phone, mail and/or email.

- Repeatedly leaving or sending victim unwanted items, presents or flowers.

- Following the person to places such as home, school or work.

---

4   Stalking Resource Center, National Center for Victims of Crime

- Harassing victim through the internet.

- Obtaining personal information about the victim by accessing public records, using internet search services, hiring private investigators, going through the victim's garbage.

- Contacting the victim's friends, family, workplace, neighbors, etc.

Summary

Confusion and the potential for miscommunication or misinterpretation of behaviors makes relationships difficult to manage, but the benefits of developing lasting and healthy relationships far outweigh the necessary work. With some commitment and communication, any worthwhile relationship can be mutually beneficial. It is essential that you carefully navigate new relationships. Whether new acquaintanceship, friendship or potential romantic relationship, respecting others and paying attention to non-verbal and verbal cues and responding accordingly will keep you on the right track and keep all parties in the safe zone!

Reference

Hussey, M. (2015) 'The absolute fail-safe way to have the "where is this going" talk.' *Cosmopolitan*. Available at www.cosmopolitan.com/sex-love/news/a41264/how-to-ask-where-relationship-going/, accessed on 31 October 2015.

Stalking Resource Center, National Center for Victims of Crime. Available at www.victimsofcrime.org/our-programs/stalking-resource-center, accessed on 4 February 2016.

Chapter 3

Let's Talk about Sex

Sexuality, Sexual Relationships and Safe Sex

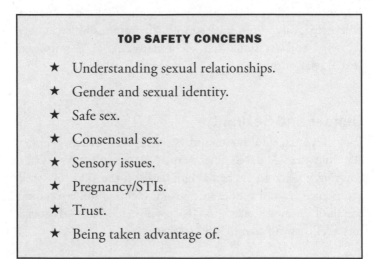

TOP SAFETY CONCERNS

★ Understanding sexual relationships.

★ Gender and sexual identity.

★ Safe sex.

★ Consensual sex.

★ Sensory issues.

★ Pregnancy/STIs.

★ Trust.

★ Being taken advantage of.

When it comes to sex and intimacy, the timing needs to be right and it cannot be rushed. I went to a party once where something physical could have happened with a girl and my friends were pressuring me. I told myself not to be naïve and not dare do anything because I was not mature enough and ready for a physical relationship with someone. I also think it is important to talk about and think about sex respectfully—not saying derogatory terms like "getting laid." Enjoy the steps and don't rush things— wait for the RIGHT thing! (Alex, young adult with ASD)

Human beings are social and sexual beings. Preferences of sexual expression vary from person to person, but the desire to engage in social relationships is very common, even among young adults on the spectrum. Although individuals with ASD are often portrayed as loners who do not want to engage in relationships, this cannot be further from the truth. In fact, many individuals with ASD both desire and experience romantic relationships,[1] and you might too! This chapter will help you better understand the responsibility, safety concerns and decisions that accompany sexual identity and sexual relationships.

Gender and Sexuality

Part of young adulthood and sexual safety includes under-standing sexual development and gender identity. While you might place less personal emphasis on the value of social acceptance around gender and sexual identity, understanding the fluid nature of these concepts will help you avoid social mistakes that can lead to safety issues.

Social Construction of Gender and Sexuality

Friends, family and popular media likely influence your beliefs about gender and sexuality (see the figure "Stereotyped sexual characteristics"). In many cultures any deviation in gender assignment or sexuality is considered wrong and can result in

---

1   Byers *et al.* (2013)

lack of social acceptance, making others the victims of hate crimes, ostracizing them or leading to depression and anxiety.

♂ Men	♀ Women
Tough demeanor	Passive
Less emotional	Emotional lability
Short hair	Long hair
Sexually attracted to females	Sexually attracted to males
Male body part	Female body parts

Stereotyped sexual characteristics

Safety Concerns

Unfortunately, identifying with a minority sexual identity or non-birth gender could have negative implications, depending on your environment. Knowing these safety concerns is important as you explore your sexuality and gender. It is especially important to understand that many people place a high value on socially constructed "normative behaviors" (i.e. heterosexuality, in this case), which drive their actions and impact their judgments.[2] This does not mean that you or your friends needs to change for other people; however, it is important for you to have an awareness of how others may perceive and treat people based on their notions of gender and sexuality.

Understanding how society responds to sexuality and gender, and more specifically how the local community and specific friends and family feel about issue of sexuality and

---

2   Rigler, Rutherford and Quinn (2005)

sexual preference, will help you navigate these oftentimes heated issues in social situations. Others' reactions and responses to discussions around gender identity and sexual orientation are largely determined by their geographical region and the convictions of their family, friends and religious beliefs. While everyone has a right to share an opinion, these conversations can become quite controversial and heated. Overall, you need to understand that sexuality is a sensitive topic and that it is not OK to use pejorative[3] and hurtful words like *fag, gay* or *homo*. Insulting and hurtful language can lead to altercations with others and can quickly escalate to physical violence. Sex and sexual orientation, while not taboo, are sensitive topics and should be discussed respectfully and among trusted others.

When individuals do identify in the sexual or gender identity minority, they have a higher chance of being bullied or harassed (see the section "Peer Victimization and Bullying" in Chapter 1 for proactive and self-defense suggestions). There are social—and even legal—repercussions against individuals who display violence or blatant discrimination against another solely by reason of gender identity and sexual orientation. If you are on the receiving end of violence because of gender identity or sexual orientation, or even how others perceive it, you should contact the local authorities. Under no circumstances is violence acceptable.

Understanding Sexuality and Gender
Sexuality
Grasping the intricacies of the physical act of sex, if you are interested in sex, will include figuring out your sexual orientation.

3　A word expressing contempt or disapproval

Sexual orientation and development can be thought of as existing on a spectrum, similar to your ASD characteristics.

Spectrum of sexual interest: non-sexual to sexual

← ─────────────────────────────────── →

Non-sexual (asexual)   Sexual

Spectrum of sexual orientation: heterosexual to homosexual

← ─────────────────────────────────── →

Heterosexual   Bisexual   Homosexual

Spectrum of sexual interest and sexual orientation

One's sexual orientation can be classified in many different ways, some are noted below.

- **Heterosexual** (attraction to opposite gender).
- **Bisexual** (attraction to both genders).
- **Homosexual** (attraction to same gender).
- **Asexual** (not sexually attracted to anyone).

Note: Keep in mind that romantic feelings may exist outside of sexual desire. It is very possible to be romantically attracted to someone but have an absence of sexual attraction at the same time. Sex and intimacy are two different things.

> I want to be able to show affection, but not necessarily in a sexual way. I think waiting and taking it slow makes it more powerful and meaningful—worth the wait. Also, people always confuse intimacy and sexual relations. I am very big on affection. It's incredible how a simple hug or kind words can be extremely uplifting. (Dave, young adult with ASD)

Gender

Gender identity can be described as the degree to which you associate with femininity and masculinity, regardless of your biological sex (male versus female). Gender is generally expressed through dress and physical appearance, and may also be characterized through the use of gender-specific pronouns. Some individuals who are assigned a certain sex at birth may feel more comfortable expressing a different gender, and may identify as transgender.

Disclosing Sexual Orientation

"Coming out" is the process through which someone discloses his or her sexual orientation to others. Disclosing sexual orientation to other people, although it may be overt in some contexts, can have significant implications, especially if the individual does not identify as heterosexual. Individuals with ASD often view themselves as a minority—you might too. Adding a minority sexual orientation or gender identity to the mix can contribute to feelings of not belonging or being different. Remember that coming out is a complex action that requires an assessment and prediction of other people's responses, including deciphering non-verbal cues, which can be difficult. Individuals who are considering coming out should identify friends and family members as trusted allies who can provide emotional support. Tip 3.1 offers questions to consider if you, or a friend, are coming out. By reviewing these questions, you can identify safe allies for support and avoid some potential safety issues by recognizing when someone is not open to the concept of a non-heterosexual relationship.

For some, "coming out" about sexual orientation/identity is a natural and stress-free process. For others, it can be fraught with anxiety and/or resistance from others. It is important to feel safe and supported throughout the process of developing your sexual identity. The following section provides guidance and considerations around "coming out."

TIP 3.1 Questions to help identify good allies

☑ Does the person say negative things about individuals who are LGBTQ+ (lesbian, gay, bisexual and transgender or people who are questioning their sexual identities)?

☑ How does the person respond to positive images of LGBTQ+ issues in the media?

☑ How does the person respond to negative images of LGBTQ+ in the media?

☑ Is he or she vocal about political LGBTQ+ issues, like marriage rights and defense from discrimination in various contexts?

Know Your Resources

Knowing about available resources ensures you are able to navigate these issues safely and confidently and address any implications. As mentioned above, identifying a support system is important. There are also local community-based centers focused on advocacy, education and support for individuals who identify as LGBTQ+. In many cases, these community centers are good resources, even if you simply want to examine these issues further without having to actually come out as non-heterosexual. Local LGBTQ+ centers often have information and resources that can help individuals navigate this process and provide support.

Sexual Relationships

> Sometimes it is difficult thinking about relationships; it seems strange because the roles are reversed from many of the relationships I see on TV in that I (the guy) am the one who moves more slowly. I have trouble understanding why everyone moves so quickly sexually and in dating. (Patrick, young adult with ASD)

Sexuality is an important part of most romantic relationships. Unfortunately, many of the stereotypes about individuals with ASD depict them as asexual or focus on sexual difficulty or problematic behavior at the expense of discussing healthy sexual development.[4] But studies show that most individuals with ASD report positive sexual relationships.[5] In fact, many of the same issues that neuro-typicals find critical to a satisfying sexual relationship will be important to you (see Critical considerations for satisfying sexual relationships).

One concern regarding relationships that individuals with ASD report is trust.

> Trust is huge. I've been a lot more trusting of people than I should have been—which is why I've stayed away from online dating. People pick up that I can be extremely naïve at times and people should be aware of this because they are especially visible targets. (Aaron, young adult with ASD)

---

4   Koller (2000)
5   Byers and Nichols (2014)

CRITICAL CONSIDERATIONS FOR
SATISFYING SEXUAL RELATIONSHIPS

- Level of interest in sex for both partners.

- Types of sexual activities you are interested in exploring.

- Level of comfort and trust with your partner.

- Extent to which your partner is comfortable with you.

- Extent to which you are relaxed with your partner.

- How your partner treats you (verbally and physically) before, during and after sex (and related activities).

- Extent to which you are physically attracted to your partner.

- Sensory differences (too much or too little sensation from touching, caressing, hugging).

Communicating about Sexual Relationships

Discuss both partners' sexual histories. It is best to ask for a couple of reasons. First, it is good to know whether one partner has an STD, and whether you still want to proceed. Second, it is a good idea to ask what someone is OK with beforehand, so you can respect their boundaries, whatever the reason for them may be. (Scott, young adult with ASD)

SOCIAL SCRIPT 3.1 NEGOTIATING A SEXUAL RELATIONSHIP: STARTING THE CONVERSATION

When you've been dating someone and things are becoming physical, it is a good idea to discuss if a sexual relationship is going to begin and the desired parameters of this part of the relationship. For example you can say:

"I know we've been dating for a while and I think we should discuss where this is going. I want to make sure that before we share any intimacy we have a discussion about sex, and that you feel respected and that I communicate with you about this."

SOCIAL SCRIPT 3.2 SEXUAL HISTORY: ENSURING SAFETY

While it is not necessary to know all of the past partners of your potential partner, it is important to ensure that they do not have any active sexually transmitted diseases/infections. Most STD/STIs do not have symptoms (or at least not symptoms that are visible). It is important that both parties be tested for all STD/STIs to reduce the likelihood of transmission. For example you can say:

"I know this isn't a comfortable topic for most, but if we are going to be in a sexual relationship we need to care about and respect each other enough to make sure we are clear of any sexually transmitted diseases. There is a free clinic that does testing, would you be willing to go together and get tested?"

Communication is essential for understanding, developing and maintaining close personal relationships. In fact, sexual and nonsexual relationship communication is associated with greater sexual satisfaction.[6] Given this, it is important for you to have the additional tools for negotiating and communicating about a sexual relationship (see Social Scripts 3.1 and 3.2).

Masturbation and Pornography

Humans are sexual beings; however, some people choose not to engage in sexual behaviors with others. This may be due to a number of reasons, including limited experience with social relationships, sensory sensitivities, relationship status (i.e., being single or in the early stages of a relationship) and/or a desire to abstain. This choice does not negate the fact that many people have innate sexual desires. You are not immune to these desires. The expression of sexual desires, either with another person or alone, can be a release of mental and emotional tension.[7]

People often choose to engage in sexual exploration and self-stimulation, in the absence of a physical relationship, as a form of sexual activity, or in addition to an existing sexual relationship. Masturbation (i.e., sexual self-stimulation) is a normal human activity that can be beneficial if conducted in a safe and healthy way.

Some people also engage in the viewing of pornography as an alternative or augmentation to other sexual activities. Because pornography is so widely accessible on the internet it is likely that you will have easy access to such content. It is important to keep in mind that the majority of images and actions viewed in pornography do not depict "real" sexual

---

6   MacNeil and Byers (2009)
7   Pukki (2003)

activity and often do not present individuals, especially females, in a positive light. Pornography can lead to reduced sexual functioning and can be addictive. There are real safety concerns about the overuse and overviewing of (or over-dependence on) pornography. The rules set out below will help keep you safe and out of potential legal or relationship trouble when it comes to pornography and masturbation.

RULES REGARDING THE USE OF PORNOGRAPHY

- Pornography uses explicit images, and those images should always be of consenting adults. If an individual has any indication that the person in the image is a minor, he or she should stop watching immediately as watching minors (any individual under the age of 18, 19 in some states) in sexual situations is illegal.

- Pornography should never be viewed on a public computer or in a public place. Anyone forced to witness this because you are watching could have grounds for legal action.

- Individuals with ASD have a tendency to become overly focused on a single interest or topic area. This can be true for the use of pornography and masturbation as well. Be mindful of the time spent on this activity, as it can overtake and have a severe impact on other things that are important in your life.

- You should not openly discuss pornography, as it may offend others.

RULES REGARDING MASTURBATION

- Right place and right time: Masturbation should always take place in complete privacy and during a time when other activities are not occurring.

- As with any activity that is enjoyable, it is possible to become over-dependent on the feeling, and a person could resort to masturbating at work or in school when other activities are a priority.

- Masturbation is a very private act and should not be discussed in public, as it may make others feel uncomfortable. In addition, masturbation should not occur where/when others may see or hear it.

- Any product of masturbation should be disposed of personally and not left behind for others to find or attend to (e.g., sheets, towels, etc.).

Safe Sex
STD/STIs

Sexual relationships can be very fulfilling, but also come with several safety concerns. First, unprotected and "protected" (abstinence is the only true method of avoiding STI/STDs) oral, vaginal and anal sex can lead to sexually transmitted diseases (STDs) or sexually transmitted infections (STIs). STDs are caused by infections that are passed from one person to another during sexual contact. When the infections cause symptoms they are referred to as STDs, and in the absence of symptoms they are called STIs. Many STD/ STIs are treatable, but some are not and result in life-long conditions that can be transmitted to future partners. It is important that you understand these conditions and how to protect yourself and your future sexual partners.

So How do People Contract STDs and STIs?

Some STIs are transmitted through vaginal fluid, seminal fluid and/or blood, while others are transmitted through skin-to-skin contact. In order to transmit most infections, such as gonorrhea, chlamydia, syphilis, trichomoniasis, HIV and hepatitis, there must be an exchange of bodily fluids. However, infections like genital warts, herpes, scabies and pubic lice can be transmitted by skin-to-skin contact and don't require sexual contact (see modes of transmission below). A condom can be a barrier for fluids but it does not eliminate all skin-to-skin contact. As a result, transmission of STIs such as herpes, HPV, syphilis, pubic lice or scabies can occur even if a condom is used.

Modes of transmission include:[8]

- sexual transmission (genital-anal, genital-genital, oral-genital/anal)

- skin-to-skin contact (i.e., kissing, non-penetrative sex, body rubbing)

- mixture of infectious body fluids (blood, semen, vaginal secretions, saliva)

- sharing of needles and other drug paraphernalia and needle stick injuries

---

8   Adapted from: www.cdc.gov/std

- from a pregnant woman to her unborn fetus or to infants during vaginal delivery or through breast milk
- infestations (scabies and pubic lice) can also be transmitted through shared clothing, bedding, linens, etc.

TIP 3.2 **How to use a condom**[9]

☑ Check the expiration date. Never use an expired condom!

☑ Open the package carefully. Teeth or long fingernails can tear the condom.

☑ If the condom doesn't have a reservoir end (small gap between head of penis and end of condom to collect semen), leave about half an inch of space at the end to collect the semen.

☑ Always use water-based or silicone-based lube with latex condoms. Never use an oil-based lube with latex condoms (this includes, baby oil, coconut oil, etc.) as it can break the condom.

☑ Do not leave condoms in hot places like in your wallet or in your car.

☑ Never reuse a condom.

---

9   Adapted from www.optionsforsexualhealth.org

So How do I Protect Myself?

According to the Centers for Disease Control (CDC), abstinence is the only true defense against STD/STIs. Second to that, condoms are the most effective method of preventing the transmission of STD/STIs. Unfortunately, condoms are not always used correctly, causing them to have little protective value, which can place you at risk of infection. For example, the risk of STI increases if the condom breaks, is reused or comes off during sex. Some STIs are also transmitted through oral sex, including herpes, gonorrhea, syphilis and HPV. Using condoms and oral dental dams as barriers is the best way to avoiding contracting an STI during oral sex. As stated before, condoms are not 100 percent effective, so advanced practice of handling and using condoms is necessary before a sexual encounter (see Tip 3.2).

Getting Tested

Anyone planning to engage in a consensual sexual relationship should be tested for STDs and STIs at a local clinic or college health service or by his or her personal doctor. You can find a provider for testing by going to certain websites.[10] Testing should be exhaustive, and include testing for HIV, gonorrhea, chlamydia, HPV, herpes type 1 and 2, hepatitis B and C, and syphilis. While testing negative for STD/STIs is a good sign that someone is free of infection, there are times when false negatives occur. This happens when testing is performed too soon after exposure. For example, someone being tested for HIV needs to be retested three to six months after the date of potential exposure, as it can take from six weeks to

---

10   www.FindSTDTest.org, www.hc-sc.gc.ca/hc-ps/dc-ma/sti-its-eng.php
      or   www.nhs.uk/Conditions/Sexually-transmitted-infections/Pages/
      Introduction.aspx

six months for the body to produce enough antibodies to be detected by the test.

Pregnancy

Another potential complication of unprotected sex is pregnancy. Contraception is not 100 percent effective. The most commonly used form of contraception from pregnancy is the use of condoms and birth control pills/injections/ devices. While these methods are almost 99 percent effective, they do fail sometimes, leading to unwanted pregnancies. If you enter into a sexual relationship you should discuss what you would do in the event of a pregnancy and make sure your sexual partner agrees.

People have a right (and a responsibility) to protect themselves and their health. While birth control pills are good safeguard against pregnancy if taken as directed, they are not an effective method to prevent STIs/STDs. While not 100 percent effective, using condoms (in addition to birth control pills or injections) is the smart thing to do. It is also a way for partners to care for themselves and one another. People who pressure others to have sex without condoms are not good partners and do not care about their partner's well-being.

Using contraception is difficult enough, with all the dos and don'ts associated with proper use. Unfortunately, knowing all of the rules of contraception is not enough. For many people, learning to discuss contraception is the toughest part. When entering a sexual relationship, it is important that you learn to negotiate boundaries, likes and dislikes, and contraception. Despite how essential this is, most people do not actually know how to navigate these discussions. With heightened emotions and libido, and potential inexperience, it is essential that these discussions occur *in advance* of the sexual encounter. The following social scripts will help you with these difficult and sometimes awkward conversations.

SOCIAL SCRIPT 3.3 DISCUSSING CONDOM USE

Discussing sexual history and claiming to be "free of disease" is not enough.

Potential resistance: "I was tested and am clean, don't you trust me?"

Suggested response: "This isn't about trust, anyone can have an STD and not even know it. Using protection is the responsible and healthy way to take care of both of us."

Sometimes people do not like the sensation of wearing a condom. It doesn't matter; it's not a preference—it's safety!

Potential resistance: "Condoms irritate my skin and it doesn't feel the same."

Suggested response: "I will only have protected sex. Sex is about more than just one sensation. We should both feel comfortable and confident during sex, and this is what makes me comfortable."

A Bad Mix: Alcohol, Drugs and Sex

Sexual activity often co-occurs with drug and alcohol use, which can lead to impulsive decisions and failure to use protection. These impulses may lead to having sex without protection or without consent. In addition to the consequences listed above (i.e., STI/STDs, pregnancy) individuals who have sex while intoxicated or under the influence might also find themselves in legal trouble, especially if one person feels they were not able to give consent fully. Consent should be received in a clear manner using words or actions that communicate a voluntary agreement to engage in the activity. *Consent is never implied* and cannot be assumed—for example, the absence of "no" does not mean "yes." Also, just because someone consented to an activity once, this does not automatically mean they want to engage in the activity again. To avoid these issues, you should never mix sex and alcohol or drugs. You should also never engage in sexual activity with someone who has been drinking or who is under the influence of drugs. People under the influence of these substances are unable to consent fully to sexual activity (see Chapter 5 for more information about drinking and sexual activity).

Sensory Issues

Some individuals with ASD experience sensory overload, and what feels good to someone else may be painful or intolerable to you. It is essential to communicate your sensory sensitivities with your partner. If you know, for example, that kissing is not a pleasurable act for you, it would be important to communicate this to your partner. This way, kissing would be something that is not part of your physical relationship. Most importantly, a satisfying sexual relationship is different for different people. Doing what makes you and your partner feel good, in a trusting and respectful manner, will result in the most satisfying physical relationship. Some people prefer to engage only in physical acts such as holding hands or cuddling. This is perfectly acceptable and no one should ever feel pressured to engage in activities that are uncomfortable or unwanted.

Physical Safety

> I put my guard down because I was told that once you are
> an adult you are good—but the opposite is true—once
> you are out of school there are a lot less people accountable
> for your safety. It's a lot more dangerous in the adult world.
> There are a lot of predators, especially when it comes to
> sexual activity. People on the spectrum need to be told
> (and have it reinforced) to be wary of talking to strangers.
> (Aaron, young adult with ASD)

Safety is paramount when deciding to enter a sexual relationship
or any relationship. While many young adults understand
the physical and medical consequences of entering a sexual
relationship (e.g., STDs/STIs or pregnancy), the need for safety
goes well beyond these issues.

Sexual Assault

Unfortunately, there are times when one person desires a
sexual relationship and the other does not. One may either
feel unable, or not be given the opportunity, to say "no." It
may be that one person is physically stronger than the other
and sex is forced, or that drugs or alcohol are used to help
reduce the resistance of the person who does not desire a
sexual relationship (e.g., use of drink spiking, date-rape drugs,
voluntary drinking). An essential tenet of a healthy sexual
relationship is that it is consensual; that is, you and your
partner mutually agree to engage in the behavior.

Emotions

When you enter a sexual relationship you are also giving a part
of your emotional self. Everyone has heard of a broken heart;

this happens when one person's emotions do not align with the other's. In a sexual relationship it may be presumed that both parties feel the same way about one another, but sometimes this is not true. At baseline, relationships tend to be very emotional. When you add sex-related components to the relationship mix, the high stakes and high emotions become more pronounced. Concerns about pregnancy, STDs and infidelity intensify these already high emotional stakes.

Summary

Entering into a sexual relationship requires personal insight into your preferences, comfort level and concerns regarding the status of a relationship before sex and an understanding of the commitment and responsibilities that come with engaging in sexual acts. It is always appropriate for you to insist that a sexual partner be tested for STD/STIs, uses protection, honors your boundaries and has the same long-term goals for the relationship. While discussing these matters may seem uncomfortable at first, any healthy relationship will embrace the space to have these adult discussions. Sex should be pleasurable and should always be consensual. If you have questions or concerns about a previous sexual encounter or a potential future relationship there are multiple resources to assist including:

- National Sexual Assault Hotline: 800.656.HOPE (4673)

- CDC National STD Hotline: (800) 227-8922

- GLBT National Hotline: 1-888-843-4564

- Rape Crisis Centres: www.rapecrisis.org.uk 0808 802 9999

- FPA: www.fpa.org.uk

- Support line: www.supportline.org.uk/problems/
  sexuality.php

References

Byers, E. and Nichols, S. (2014) 'Sexual satisfaction of high functioning adults with Autism Spectrum Disorder.' *Sex and Disability 32,* 365–382.

Byers, E., Nichols, S., Voyer, S. and Reilly, G. (2013) 'Sexual well being of a community sample of high functioning adults on the autism spectrum who have been in a romantic relationship.' *Autism 17,* 418–433.

Centers for Disease Control (2015) *CDC Fact Sheet: Information for Teens: Staying Healthy and Preventing STDs.* Atlanta, GA: Centers for Disease Control. Available at www.cdc.gov/std/life-stages-populations/stdfact-teens.htm, accessed 31 October 2015.

Koller, R. (2000) 'Sexuality and adolescents with autism.' *Sexuality and Disability 18,* 2, 125–135.

MacNeil, S. and Byers, E. S. (2009) 'Role of sexual self-disclosure in the sexual satisfaction of long-term heterosexual couples.' *Journal of Sex Research 46,* 1–12.

Pukki, H. (2003) 'Developing expressions of sexuality: The perspective and experiences of able autistic people'. *Good Autism Practice Journal 4,* 2, 60–65.

Rigler, M., Rutherford, A. amd Quinn, E. (2015) *Turning Skills and Strengths into Careers for Young Adults with Autism Spectrum Disorder: The BASICS College Curriculum.* London: Jessica Kingsley Publishers.

Chapter 4

Safely Navigating the Web

Social Media and Online Safety

TOP SAFETY CONCERNS

★ Social media protocol.

★ "Friending" others.

★ Using LinkedIn appropriately.

★ Online relationships, "online dating."

★ Online "cyber" bullying.

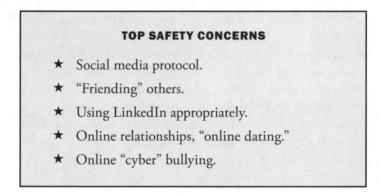

Social media

Social Media Protocol

> I only use FB and only "friend" people I know in real life. I also make sure my privacy settings are strict—only friends vs. friends of friends. Finally, I only put things on my FB wall that I would say to anyone! (Neal, young adult with ASD)

Our society has an innate social structure that involves unwritten rules, cues, identifiers and roles. Within this social structure, you might become confused by the non-verbal cues and body language used to deliver a variety of messages. Non-verbal communication becomes even more complicated with the addition of social media and its use in everyday life. Social media includes a variety of websites and apps that are used to connect people online through chatting, blogging, photo blogging and other forms of networking as reflected in the image above. This includes sites such as Facebook that allow users to share status updates, share pictures and let people know their current location by "checking in." Instagram and Tumblr are other common social media apps that people use to share pictures. Other social media like Twitter and Vine limit the user to very brief text (i.e., 140 characters or fewer) or video. Finally, Pinterest is a popular app that allows the user to share creative ideas, photos and projects that they find interesting. While sharing pictures, videos and other information can be a fun way to connect with others, it is vital to keep in mind that once shared, videos and images *stay* online—forever. Once media is posted to the internet it can always be found, even if you remove or "erase" it. Further, they are in the public domain—meaning they no longer belong to you—and can be misused or manipulated in ways that can be embarrassing, harmful or even unsafe.

Social media is used to socialize with people, practice relationship building, develop interests and explore and express identity. Most young adults maintain at least one social media profile. Social media offers an avenue to build and sustain relationships in a less stressful way, removing the need for face-to-face contact and while this form of socialization can be a great tool to increase communication with others locally and worldwide, there are some cautions that you should note when you go online.

> It's been a journey to get to this point. For three quarters of my high school years, I had no friends. I wasn't aware of social media back then. Getting into social media has helped me connect with others and has been the key to social relationships. Invitations to parties and events were *through* Facebook and other social media outlets. These invites have solidified my social life and allowed me to enhance my friendships with others, both in person and online. (Dave, young adult with ASD)

A recent study suggests that people who choose to engage in social media relationships and those who engage in social media are more likely to have close friends.[1] As you begin the process of interacting with others through social media, it is important to discuss potential safety concerns. The number one concern is that anything put online today can ruin your future tomorrow. You should be very careful about what you post and what is posted about you. Acquaintances, friends, family members, coworkers/employers, future boyfriend/girlfriends and even the police have access to what you post online. Something you may find funny today may interfere with something important to you in the future, like a potential job. Understanding privacy settings on social media sites and maintaining strict privacy settings is critical. Many social

---

1   Mazurek (2013)

media sites change default privacy settings without informing members, so be alert to how privacy setting are assigned and maintained. Without limiting who has access, anyone can see your information and pictures. Social media accounts can be hacked (i.e., entered into by someone with computer savvy that is not you), so you should protect and change your password often. Also, if someone is communicating with you via social media and something doesn't seem right (e.g., they are acting weird or asking for inappropriate things), do not respond. It may be that a friend's account was hacked or an online friend should no longer be trusted (see Tip 4.1).

TIP 4.1 **Proactive behaviors to ensure a safer experience online**

☑ Set privacy setting so only people you approve can see your pictures and protected information.

☑ Social media profiles can be hacked, so protect yours with a solid password that you change often.

☑ Avoid friending "friends of friends" whom you have not actually met.

☑ Don't link your phone number or email to your public profile.

☑ If someone has "unfriended you," "blocked you" or is not replying to any of your messages or wall posts stop contacting them.

☑ Don't ever post something you don't want available to anyone in the future.

☑ Do not post inappropriate pictures online or via text. A simple screenshot can archive these images to be used for hurtful reasons in the future.

☑ Do not engage in cyber sexting (i.e., texting messages or pictures of a sexual nature to someone else) or anything similar through video feeds. These can be recorded or a screenshot can be created for hurtful reasons.

☑ Protect yourself and disengage from the social media outlet in the instant you start to feel bullied or degraded.

☑ Do not say anything in an online forum that you would not say face to face.

☑ Finally, always project an accurate picture of who you are, but recognize that not everyone does this.

Although social media by nature is "social," some people who use social media are very particular about their privacy and being tagged in photos, being friended and having their posts shared. Therefore, you should be conservative in your approaches to social media. In fact, it is often best to let others take the lead on connecting with you in these domains. There are a few strict rules, however, you can follow to ensure proper social media etiquette is practiced. First, "friending" someone you don't know, but who is a friend of a friend, could be considered an invasion of privacy (see Social Script 4.1). Everyone has the right to control his or her information. Contacting someone via social media can sometimes be misinterpreted as harassment. As such, you should avoid re-adding or sending direct messages to people who have blocked you or who are not responding to your inquiries (see the section "Harassment" in Chapter 2). Also, keep in mind that people can readily hide or even be dishonest about their online identity—just because someone says they are 18 years old and a female, this does not mean that they really are. If you have not met them in person they could be someone completely different than who they portray online.

SOCIAL SCRIPT 4.1 RESPONDING TO REQUESTS FOR PRIVATE INFORMATION

Someone with whom you have been communicating on Facebook for over a year starts saying things that don't sound the same as what you have talked about previously, which makes you question with whom you are interacting. Finally, he asks you to send him a picture of yourself in a private message and you do not feel comfortable doing so.

"(Insert name) this doesn't sound like how you have talked in the past. I have really liked getting to know you, but this makes me feel very uncomfortable. I don't know why you want my picture and I am very careful about who I give pictures of myself to. I hope that you are not offended, but I am not interested in sharing pictures right now."

Social media can be a great forum for you to connect with others with similar interests. Similar to the now ancient practice of being pen pals, social media allows you to develop various forms of relationships with people from around the world. This "virtual" form of relationship building can help you through the often difficult stages of forming relationships by relieving some of the pressures of social rules (e.g., eye contact, reading facial cues, personal space). These benefits however do not come without a cost. It is imperative that you have an awareness of the potential safety concerns and possible missteps regarding social media and that you diligently follow the outlined social media protocols to ensure your safety online.

"Friending" Others

> In real life (IRL)—only friend someone that you know IRL; do not give out any identifiable information online. (Hikarih, young adult with ASD)

A significant change to the social world is the influx of social media. People easily become defined by how many "friends" they have on Facebook, how many "followers" they have on Instagram or how many "likes" they can get on a picture. This is quickly becoming the new yardstick by which young adults measure social standing. These new social structures create their own layers of confusion and new social difficulties. At the core of the confusion are the definition of friendship and the notion of "friending" people or allowing people to "follow" you even though you may not know them very well—even though the identified "friends" on your social media profiles may or may not be true friends and may instead be acquaintances. You should carefully separate the concept of online friends compared with genuine friends and make sure you understand that your worth is not measured in "likes." For example, some of your friends may have upwards of 1,000 "friends" and thousands of "followers" with hundreds of "likes" on every picture. The reality of the social media phenomena is that the number of people you follow, or who follow you, is not an accurate display of true friendships (see the figure "Authenticity of relationships"). Also, social media is rarely a completely accurate portrayal of people's personalities. People will only post their best attributes, accomplishments, photos and ideas, not the areas with which they struggle. Approaching social media in an educated way and discussing the differences between real "friends" and social media "friends" can help you understand social media and the responsible way to use this medium. It is also wise to remember that using social media as a means to compare yourself with others is inaccurate and can lead to compromised self-esteem.

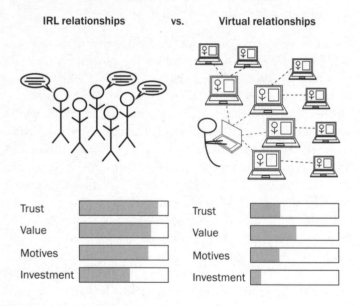

Authenticity of relationships

While a few virtual relationships may carry the same authenticity as IRL relationships, when the web of virtual connections expands, the authenticity of those relationships decreases.

I used to put a lot more effort into my online relationships. I preferred to be by myself doing my own thing. I didn't like what other people my age liked. I didn't like parties, drinking, etc. Online, people depended on me and always talked about being depressed or upset about something in their life and I was the one that could make them smile. I felt a lot of responsibility and it started making me really tired because I wasn't getting anything in return from them. Over the past year, I have grown up a lot and decided to put more effort into my real-life relationships. I stopped spending so much time online and starting spending more time with friends in my own town. I feel more supported now. When people support me too, the relationships feel more real. (KT, young adult with ASD)

Using social media as a responsible social outlet can help you practice the art of communication through avenues that may be less threatening than face-to-face interaction with another person. Online, people don't have to worry about eye contact, standing too close, talking too loudly or quietly or coming up with a response quickly. In this environment people can choose the frequency and time of interactions and can analyze responses before sending them. In addition, relationships can be built through the simple act of "liking" a picture or comment. Identifying shared interests in this way can be the start of an authentic friendship.

Once some social commonalities (i.e., interests or points of view) have emerged with another person and you feel comfortable interacting online, the next step is developing a relationship outside of the internet. By simply developing a social script and reviewing it with a trusted friend or parent before sending a message online, you can begin the process of developing authentic friendships based on shared interests discovered online (see Social Script 4.2).

SOCIAL SCRIPT 4.2 MEETING PEOPLE ONLINE

While commenting back and forth with someone on social media about an experience at a convention, you notice that you are sharing vivid stories and discussing characters in detail. You know that this person goes to the same school that you do and you make the decision to try to meet up in person.

"(Insert name) it was really fun talking with you online about the convention and the characters that you like from (insert details). We go to the same school, so I think it would be fun to get together after school sometime and talk about the conventions. Would you be interested in meeting sometime at the school?"

Using LinkedIn and Online Professional Networking Appropriately

As you begin your job or career search, a vital aspect of this search process is professional networking. Using social media as a networking tool can be highly valuable. Sites such as LinkedIn allow you to highlight your professional strengths and skills. Setting up a profile on LinkedIn takes very little time and is a great alternative to the traditional networking activities that tend to be highly social in nature and involve talking face to face with people. By sharing your resume and getting endorsements from respected people, you can bypass many of the initial stages of the recruitment process and professionals can focus directly on your strengths and skill set. Of course, understanding the rules of using a social media platform for employment connections is critical to ensuring you don't commit a "faux pas" in this area.

Relationships on LinkedIn are termed "connections" as opposed to "friends" or "followers," and these connections are professional in nature—not personal. You can add connections by reading the profiles of others in a similar area or by joining groups in your area of expertise. This online professional network reduces the need to engage in social interaction (e.g., small talk), but still provides the benefit of professional networking.

LinkedIn is very different than other social media sites in that it is focused primarily on the professional lives of the users. This is *not* a site where people share intimate or overly personal information or photos of a personal nature. This is also *not* the place to share your religious or political views, family issues, work difficulties or anything that could be perceived as unprofessional or controversial. This particular social media site can be viewed as a living and evolving professional resume. A potential employer has access to anything posted on this site; therefore, it is imperative that you maintain a high level of professionalism through your profile (see Tip 4.2 and the figure "Differences between Facebook and LinkedIn").

	Facebook	LinkedIn	
Personal pictures	Yes	No	LinkedIn allows you to post a profile picture. Make sure this photo is professional.
Update status	Yes	No	
Post job-related news	Yes	Yes	Avoid mentioning salary or slandering comments.
Comments/photos about your weekend	Yes	No	
Like statuses/photos	Yes	Yes	LinkedIn allows you to like and share professional posts made by others. Be mindful of sharing posts regarding controversial issues on LinkedIn.
List professional skills	No	Yes	
Contact potential employers	No	Yes	
Share funny videos	Yes	No	
Post your resume	No	Yes	
Update your profile	Yes	Yes	It is good practice to make a habit of updating your profile every three months or as major life events happen.

	Facebook	LinkedIn	
Chat with others	Yes	Yes	
Endorse others	No	Yes	
Post professionally relevant articles	Yes	Yes	
Connecting with people you do not know personally	No	Yes	Professionally connecting with people you do not know directly, but who may be in your career field, can help you build your professional network. This is called networking. Keep this connection professional; it is not personal.
Play gaming apps	Yes	No	
Discuss relationship status	Yes	No	
Invite others to events	Yes	Yes	Only use LinkedIn as a professional development tool.

Differences between Facebook and LinkedIn

TIP 4.2 Developing your LinkedIn profile summary

The very first step in developing a LinkedIn profile is writing a professional summary. This is a brief amount of information that is packed with details. By reading this summary, others can gain an understanding of one's professional achievements and goals. The following is an example of a professional summary on LinkedIn.

I am a goal-oriented person who strives for equality for all people. I love program development, which involves programs that encourage people with disabilities to fully participate in all that life has to offer. I am an advocate, leader, teacher, and squeaky wheel when I need to be.

Someone once wrote that to be a good leader in higher education, you have to be a dove, a dragon and a diplomat all at the same time. I tend to live my professional life as a diplomat—always negotiating on behalf of people with disabilities. When people treat others with disabilities in a discriminatory fashion, I can quickly become a dragon. The thing that makes me a dove is what drives my passion every single day. Working with the amazingly talented and honest with ASD. This is a daily challenge to become a better professional but the rewards are immense.

Meeks, Masterson and Westlake (2015) discuss the unemployment statistics for young adults with ASD and the need to use sites like LinkedIn to network professionally. By interacting with others about your strengths and skills in a non-threatening and online manner, the social difficulties associated with ASD are reduced, while your strengths are highlighted. When used properly LinkedIn can be a positive employment tool.

Etiquette for Using LinkedIn[2]

- **Use connections carefully**—Success on LinkedIn relies heavily on reputation. Be careful when asking for or making a connection.

- **Always tell the truth**—When discussing work history and accomplishments, be honest. One of the most difficult things to overcome is professional dishonesty.

- **Don't gossip**—Don't spread any company or personal gossip through LinkedIn. A potential employer will not want to hire someone who talks negatively about a previous employer.

- **Be professional**—LinkedIn is used mainly for professional networking. So, stay professional at all times. Use other sites like Facebook for personal posts.

- **Be mindful of who has access**—Current bosses, coworkers and potential employers have access to the information on LinkedIn. When making a substantial change to a profile, it is wise to notify these important people ahead of time.

---

2   Hill (2015)

Online Relationships, "Online Dating"

> Try to meet in person for the first time someplace neutral
> like a coffee shop and preferably somewhere public. This
> is both for your own safety and to put the other person
> at ease. Remember they don't know you and are probably
> just as concerned about safety as you are. Things like
> going on a canoe trip for two, or going to see a movie, can
> wait. I've actually learned this the hard way. I've definitely
> suggested those kinds of activities while online as a first
> date. And, in person, it turns out to be really awkward.
> (Scott, young adult with ASD)

One in every ten Americans (11% of American adults) utilize
dating sites or mobile apps for dating.[3] In fact, online dating
is one of the leading ways to meet a romantic partner. Many
sites are available, but a few of the most well-known sites
include eHarmony, Match, JDate and ChristianMingle.
Online dating offers you the opportunity to meet someone in a
non-threatening manner without the face-to-face interactions
that can sometimes be challenging. It also provides an
opportunity to meet others in a format that includes less
social demands (e.g., eye contact, non-verbal body language)
and in a manner that allows for more self-monitoring and
planned versus spontaneous communication, particularly
when connecting with someone for the first time. Individuals
with ASD discussed some benefits of online dating, including
"reading about the other person to see if I want to talk to them"
and the reduced "social anxiety and sensory sensitivities"
that make online dating easier than traditional dating.[4] For
those who approach relationships or coupling with a more

---

3   Smith and Duggan (2013)
4   Roth and Gillis (2015) p.138

analytical/logical approach, online dating can also provide a more pragmatic way to find a partner by focusing in on desired character traits and commonalities as opposed to instinct and reading emotional cues. Another benefit to online dating is the convenience of meeting a number of potential partners from the comfort and safety of your own home. Online dating can open up an entire world of potential partners from all over the country or even the world; however, access of this nature presents potential safety concerns alongside the benefits.

As with any online exchange, dating online comes with safety concerns. Unfortunately, you might be at risk of victimization.[5] Some individuals with ASD are exceptionally trusting and may be prone to believing everything about a person based on their online profile. Again, not everyone is honest and anyone can create an online profile that is not representative of his or her actual persona. More worrisome is the fact that people may enter online dating sites with less than honorable intentions. Some people are intentionally hoping to deceive others to gain financial or sexual benefits and it can be difficult to discern someone who should be trusted from someone who should not.

Online Safety

Risk management is the name of the game when dating online. Unfortunately, people can represent themselves falsely online. In fact, in the recent survey of individuals with ASD regarding online dating, the biggest safety concern was "other people misrepresenting themselves."[6] As well, the conversation

---

5   Roth and Gillis (2015)
6   Roth and Gillis (2015)

around meeting up can be difficult to broach, especially for young adults who are shy (see Social Script 4.3).

Meeting people online can be scary and you do need to be safe. When deciding to meet up in person after meeting online there are a few safety tips you should follow—these are explained in the following sections.

FACT CHECKING

A good place to begin once you determine that you'd like to meet the person outside of the "virtual" world of online dating is to *find out their real name and do some fact checking about the person (i.e, job, city, etc.)*. After getting a person's full name, you should *confirm the person's identity*. Many people do this through LinkedIn. Remember, however, that people can also make up false LinkedIn profiles, so having a profile on this site that matches what they tell you online still does not guarantee safety. Also, people can see each time you view them, therefore, multiple views may seem aggressive or odd or may be considered stalking. You can use the information on LinkedIn to verify that the person is indeed real and works at a particular organization by looking at the organization's website, which usually lists employees. **Do not call a person's place of employment**—doing so would violate a social norm and be viewed as intrusive. When checking facts about potential people of interest, you should be careful not to do too much fact checking. Checking a site for the person's name and information, then validating with one other site, should be enough information to confirm the person's identity.

Another safety precaution when arranging an in-person meeting with someone you met online is to *arrange your own transportation*, getting to and from the meeting alone. *Always meet in a crowded public place* and have plenty of people around when first meeting someone. It is also a good idea to let at least one other person know the meeting location, timetable and name of the person. Also, *set a check-in time* with a friend. Have a friend call or check in via text and have two words prearranged—the first a *safety word* to be used if you feel uncomfortable and second an *all-clear word* to be used if you feel safe. If you use the safety word, your friend will know that you are uncomfortable and can come and meet you and arrange for you to get home safely. If you use the all-clear word, they will know that you are feeling safe—this allows your friend to relax a bit and know that you feel comfortable on your date. Finally, someone should *ensure you arrive home safely*—this could be the same friend or another person, like a roommate, parent or sibling. *Never go home with a person you barely know* regardless of how comfortable you feel. In today's world it is not safe to go home with a stranger—and after meeting one time the person is very much still a stranger (see Tip 4.3).

SOCIAL SCRIPT 4.3 MEETING UP IN PERSON

A person you met online and with whom you have been interacting with for several months says that she wants to meet you in person. You are a little uncomfortable, but really want to meet her. You have a lot in common and have enjoyed the online relationship so far so you decide you would like to meet up but with some guidelines in place.

"(Insert name) I would really like to meet you and see if we have a connection. Because we have not met in person before, I would like to meet in a public place so both of us can be comfortable. Let's meet for lunch at (insert a busy restaurant location) so we can get to know each other better."

TIP 4.3 Safety: online dating "dos"

☑ Find out their real and full name.

☑ Confirm the person's identity.

☑ Arrange your own transportation.

☑ Always meet in a crowded public place.

☑ Set a check-in time.

☑ Establish a safety word with a friend.

☑ Establish an all-clear word with a friend.

☑ Ensure that you arrive home safely.

☑ Never go home with a person you barely know.

BUILDING A SAFE ONLINE DATING PROFILE

There are other considerations before deciding to date online that could further protect your interests and identity (see Tip 4.4).

TIP 4.4 Building a safe profile

☑ Never use your real name online or part of your real name.

☑ Do not use the same picture that you use on other public websites like LinkedIn. Google can now search by photo and someone could search Google using your profile picture and find out your identify.

☑ Withhold certain demographic information (your exact town, street, place of work, etc.).

☑ Don't ever give someone access to your email, password, bank account, etc.

☑ Be wary of individuals who do not have US citizenship and talk about marriage.

To Disclose or Not to Disclose

> I want to be honest with people about my challenges, but I don't want to scare them off. (Patrick, young adult with ASD)

Disclosing any vulnerability to a romantic interest can be scary. It can be especially concerning to disclose a diagnosis when another's perceptions of that diagnosis are unknown and can range from being highly informed to not being informed at all. Further, an individual's perception of a specific diagnosis can be especially skewed, either negatively or positively. As Scott states in the quote below, he would rather wait to disclose and allow the individual to get to know him before adding a layer of information that may negatively impact perceptions of him. Everyone has quirks, preferences and idiosyncrasies about them that manifest over time. Most people would not walk into a first date and reveal that they get really crabby if the house isn't perfectly clean or that they have a tendency to want to know where their significant other is at all times. They would, instead, allow this to unfold as part of a natural conversation about their characteristics and traits when the topic was specific to that area.

> I do not indicate that I have been diagnosed with autism on my online dating profile. I've done it before, and it is not a good idea. It opens you up to people's preconceived notions about autism and gets in the way of them getting to know me on their own. I oftentimes don't mention it on a first date either since that can have the same effect. (Scott, young adult with ASD)

While there are strong arguments for not disclosing too soon, not disclosing can set you up for failure. What if you don't disclose? A potential risk of not disclosing is having someone misinterpret your behavior. The most common misinterpretations include assuming disinterest or that someone has an aloof or narcissistic personality, but can also include some more alarming things like drug use or emotional issues. Disclosing can be wise and especially important if you have specific triggers like noise, temperature, food and touch/textures—these are often outside of your control during a date.

Cyberbullying

All too often, individuals with ASD are the victims of bullying. Whether being teased in elementary school, physically mistreated in middle school or pranked in high school, bullying is far too rampant among this population. Because they are often confused by social rules and mistreated by others, people with ASD tend to resort to online social spaces to interact with others. This allows for the engagement with other people without the need for managing the complicated social rules that exist in various situations. Whether engaging in online chat rooms or online gaming, people must be aware of the potential for what we refer to as cyberbullying.

Cyberbullying includes using technology to harass, tease or embarrass another person through text messages, social media or online gaming and is destructive on many levels. When being bullied in person, an individual can escape by leaving the situation. With cyberbullying, there is no escape. A bully can send a mean text, post an embarrassing picture or tweet from an account simulating the victim at any time and the victim can be harassed even while he or she is sitting in the safety of his or her bedroom.

Methods to Deal with Cyberbullying

Two well-known apps to reduce cyberbullying are listed below. While one works through notification to the authorities, the other works by providing the opportunity for the poster to rethink their decision to post something that might be hurtful or inappropriate.

STOPIT

STOPit is a mobile app that can be used by campuses or places of employment to help protect their students/employees. It offers an opportunity to report unwanted or inappropriate contact or bullying. It can also connect the individual to a crisis counselor or can press a panic button alerting campus security and providing an exact GPS location of the individual in danger.

RETHINK

ReThink is an approach designed to stop bullying proactively, before it begins. When someone posts a mean-spirited message on social media, the ReThink software identifies offensive posts and sends a message to the user asking them to reconsider their decision to post this material. The research around this software suggests that when prompted to "ReThink" their decision, the posting party changes their minds 93 percent of the time.[7]

ReThink, unlike victim-centered applications, places the onus on the poster to stop and reconsider their actions. The software quite literally asks the poster to pause, review and reconsider their decisions on social media. In this way, young adults self-monitor their behavior and learn to make better choices.

TIP 4.5 Defense against cyberbullying

☑ **Save all communication**: Take a screen shot of the communication that includes a date/time stamp (photo with your phone or screen shot from the computer). This way, if you have to file a report with the police or other agency you have a visual record of the communication.

☑ **Don't respond**: When someone is bullying you online do not respond—this only fuels the fire. Also, anything you post on a social media site can be captured and used against you.

☑ **Deactivate accounts**: Consider taking a vacation from social media.

☑ **Change passwords**: You should change all passwords every six months or so to reduce the likelihood of someone getting your personal information and using it against you.

---

7 Statistics found on ReThink website www.rethinkwords.com

☑ **Contact the web host**: If the bullying is happening on a social media site, contact the site host and report the problem. Social media sites like Facebook have automatic reporting/blocking features to ensure users are not harassed.

Summary

The internet has become a large part of our day-to-day life. We meet people, do business, connect with previous classmates, make professional connections and play games with people from around the world online. The use of technology has expanded our connections across the globe and allowed for more relationships to be built with people from various cultures and geographic locations. However, along with these benefits come some cautions. When using the online platform to interact with others, it is vital that you protect yourself by developing some safety strategies that are in line with the information that has been discussed in this chapter. Whether you are accessing social media to build your relationship bank, share pictures, build a social network or develop personal relationships, the most important aspect of these interactions must be to keep yourself safe.

References

Benford, P. and Standen, P. (2009) 'The internet: A comfortable communication medium for people with Asperger syndrome (AS) and high functioning autism (HFA).' *Journal of Assistive Technologies, 3*, 44–53.

Childwise (2015) *Childwise Monitor Report 2-13-14: Digital Lives.* Norwich: Childwise. Available at www.childwise.co.uk/uploads/3/1/6/5/31656353/childwise_press_release_-_technology.pdf, accessed on 4 December 2015.

Heasley, S. (2013) *For Boys with Autism, Video Gaming can be Problematic.* Available at www.theatlantic.com/technology/archive/2012/10/what-an-academic-who-wrote-her-dissertation-on-trolls-thinks-of-violentacrez/263631/, accessed on 4 February 2016.

Lonie, N. (2015) *Online Safety for Children and Teens on the Autism Spectrum: A Parent's and Carer's Guide*. London: Jessica Kingsley Publishers.

Mazurek, M. (2013) 'Social media use among adults with autism spectrum disorders.' *Computers in Human Behavior 29*, 1709–1714.

Meeks, L., Masterson, T. and Westlake, G. (2015)' Career Connect: A collaborative employment resource model for serving students with ASD in higher education.' *Career Planning and Adult Development Journal 31*, 4.

Rigler, M., Rutherford, A. and Quinn, E. (2015) *Career Goals and Job-hunting Strategies for Young Adults with ASD: The BASICS college curriculum*. London: Jessica Kingsley Publishers.

Roth, M. and Gillis, J. (2015). '"Convenience with the click of a mouse": A survey of adults with autism spectrum disorder on online dating.' *Journal of Sex and Disability 33*, 133–150.

Smith, A. and Duggan, M. (2013) *Online Dating and Relationships*. Washington, DC: Pew Research Center Internet, Science and Technology. Available at www.pewinternet.org/2013/10/21/online-dating-relationships/, accessed on 1 November 2015.

PART TWO

Health Concerns in Adulthood

Chapter 5

Drinking and Drugs

Danger Zone!

TOP SAFETY CONCERNS

★ Lack of knowledge about drinking/drugs.

★ Hangovers, blackout and alcohol poisoning.

★ Interactions with prescription medication.

★ Driving under the influence.

★ Spiking drinks.

★ Peer pressure.

Drinking in moderation has been OK for me because I know my limits. I grew up with a family who drank responsibly and taught me to do the same. What is toughest for me is being with friends who are drinking and acting out of control. When I was in college, so many people would get drunk to the point of getting sick, passing out or doing regrettable things. It seemed like drinking was all they wanted to do, but because I didn't, I either felt alone or pressure to do things I didn't feel comfortable doing. For me, it's all about moderation— usually sticking to only one drink, never drinking and driving, and drinking with safe people in safe places. I don't know why anyone would want to get so drunk that they put their lives or the lives of others in jeopardy. (Anonymous, young adult with ASD)

In Chapter 1 we discussed the benefits of socialization. Unfortunately, for young adults, socialization often centers on drinking and drug use. Consideration of the legal and safety factors associated with drinking and drug use is essential. Drinking is illegal in the US for individuals under the age of 21, and recreational drugs like marijuana, heroin and cocaine are illegal in most states (regardless of age). If you have any significant communication difficulties or executive functioning challenges (i.e. planning, organizing, problem solving, maintaining attention and focus), experimentation with drugs and alcohol should generally be avoided. Additionally, if you are on medications that have the potential to interact with drugs and alcohol you should completely avoid their use.

> It is important to educate teens and young adults about drugs and alcohol through facts, not fear. Have conversations about the ways in which medication with alcohol and drugs do not mix well. Educate the person on the autism spectrum about the nature of drugs such as the fact that alcohol is a depressant. It is found that sometimes alcohol can make medications stronger, weaker, ineffective or harmful. It is important to avoid mixing them when possible. (Beth Thompson, Milestones Autism Resources Teen/Adult Services Manager, social worker with specialization in young adults with ASD)

While it is less common for young adults with ASD to attend social events with drugs and alcohol regularly, understanding the potential consequences of alcohol and drug use is critical, especially given the naivety of many individuals on the spectrum. You should be aware that social events often include alcohol, tobacco and other recreational drugs. While you may decide to avoid drug and alcohol use at these social events, you *cannot* control the behavior and choices of others, who may decide to engage in risk-taking behaviors related to drug and alcohol use. Therefore, it is essential to have a basic level of drug and alcohol education to protect yourself and others around you.

THINGS TO BE AWARE OF WHEN OUT AND DRINKING

- Educate yourself about alcohol.

- Ensure you have a safe and sober ride home.

- Have a buddy and look after one another.

- Check to make sure you did not leave anything behind (jacket, cell phone).

- Make sure you are not leaving without your friends (remember that "buddy" we talked about).

- Make sure (if you gave your credit card to the bartender as a tab) to get your credit card before you leave.

The young adult population is traditionally an "at-risk" group, according to the *Journal of the American Medical Association*,[1] and people tend to drink the most in their late teens and twenties. Alcohol is the most commonly used and abused

---

1   Naimi *et al.* (2003)

drug among teens and young adults in the US.[2] Statistically, one in five teens is a problem drinker,[3] so even if someone is not a drinker, this will likely still impact them.

Using Alcohol as a Coping Strategy

> Sometimes I wish I liked the taste of alcohol. I think it would relax me and help me fit in better. Not drinking is just one more thing that makes me different from everybody. (Erica, young adult with ASD)

A lot of young adults turn to alcohol as a way to "cope" with other issues like social anxiety or depression, while some people drink to escape the confines of other issues like anxiety, depression and stress. Given the comorbidities (two or more psychological or medical conditions occurring together) present with most autism spectrum disorders (e.g., depression, anxiety, etc.), you might find alcohol use to be a tempting way to cope with mental health concerns.

If you struggle to fit in socially, alcohol might be viewed as a social fix. Since alcohol reduces inhibition, it can make you feel more "bold" or "confident" when interacting with others. As well, you might drink to "fit in" with the crowd, thinking that if you participate in the ritualistic behavior of your peers you will be more readily accepted. Because of the symptoms of ASD, you may tend to be socially naïve and eager to please, which makes you more vulnerable to peer pressure when people tell you to "just try it!"

It is important to realize that when you drink you may begin to violate social norms, since your inhibition is

2   Center for Disease Control, Fact-Sheets Underage Drinking
3   Substance Abuse and Mental Health Services Administration (2013)

reduced. You might not like to drink alone and would then be more likely to try and pressure others to drink because you are drinking. It may also help to consider that when you are drinking you are likely not in a clear state of mind—and could forget the encounter and/or be easily distracted by something else. In general, you should avoid situations where people are drinking heavily and should stick to your decisions about whether to drink. In the end, anyone who is pressuring others to drink or do anything else outside of their comfort zone is not a true friend. While the tendency to use this "peer pressure" to drink decreases significantly with age (peaking in high school and college), it is important that you have a prepared script (see Social Script 5.1) for when and if people offer you a drink or recreational drug.

The associated problem is that drinking itself typically makes you less inhibited and more impulsive and un-coordinated. It is also extremely difficult to practice good decision-making and utilize coping skills when you are under the influence of alcohol. When drinking, you are more likely to disregard your own safety and the safety of others (e.g., driving while intoxicated, trying other drugs that you were not intending to, engaging in risky sexual behavior, etc.), all of which come with serious consequences.

HOW MUCH IS TOO MUCH?

I wish I had known about hangovers. I went to the hospital once because I was so sick I thought it was food poisoning. I wasn't able to relate the two (drinking and then feeling sick several hours later). By the time I realized I had drank too much I was way too intoxicated. I have dampened sensitivities to a lot of things like noise, alcohol, etc. Just be aware that people on the spectrum have to be aware that things might affect them differently. (Aaron, young adult with ASD)

Blood alcohol concentration (BAC) (the measurement of alcohol concentration in the blood) is the term frequently used to quantify medically how much alcohol an individual has consumed (see Table 5.1).

Note: Some BAC monitoring devices (e.g., breathalyzers) are sold publically. Some parents and young adults make the decision to invest in a device to carry in their car. This may allow yourself and others to make more informed decisions about driving and drinking in general. Of course a BAC monitor should not be the only determining factor in deciding how much to drink or whether or not to drive, but it can be a informative and educational tool at a reasonable cost, considering the cost of driving under the influence (DUI) of alcohol or drugs, or related consequences like binge drinking, blackouts or alcohol poisoning that can lead to injury or death.

SOCIAL SCRIPT 5.1 DECLINING A DRINK

The following dialogue provides you with an example interaction in which one person is mildly pressuring someone to have a drink. Also provided are several examples of ways to conversationally respond if someone is pressuring you to drink.

Graham: "Hey, you want a beer?"

Jimmy: "No thanks..." (pick one of the following):

- I am driving.

- I hate the taste of alcohol.

- I have a test tomorrow (or a big paper).

- I have to work early tomorrow.

- I am so tired, a drink would put me to sleep.

Graham: "Aww, c'mon man, just one beer. Don't be a baby!"

Jimmy: "Like I said, no thanks."

Table 5.1 Levels of BAC and respective effects		
Blood alcohol concentration	Typical effects	Effects on driving
.02%	Some loss of judgment Relaxation Slight body warmth Altered mood	Decline in visual functions (rapid tracking of a moving target) Decline in ability to perform two tasks at the same time (divided attention)
.05%	Exaggerated behavior May have loss of small-muscle control (e.g., focusing your eyes) Impaired judgment Usually good feeling Lowered alertness Release of inhibition	Reduced coordination Reduced ability to track moving objects Difficulty steering Reduced response to emergency driving situations
.08%	Muscle coordination becomes poor (e.g., balance, speech, vision, reaction time and hearing) Harder to detect danger Judgment, self-control, reasoning and memory are impaired	Concentration Short-term memory loss Speed control Reduced information processing capability (e.g., signal detection, visual search) Impaired perception
.10%	Clear deterioration of reaction time and control Slurred speech, poor coordination and slowed thinking	Reduced ability to maintain lane position and brake appropriately

(Source: Centers for Disease Control 2015)

Unfortunately, it is very difficult to measure your BAC outside of the medical and legal arena, therefore you have to monitor closely your alcohol intake and the factors relevant to BAC such as: the amount of alcohol in each drink (based on volume and type of drink—see Table 5.2); the number of drinks consumed in a specific period of time; your tolerance level, height and weight; potential medication interactions; and whether or not you have a full or empty stomach. Many people who experiment with alcohol have difficulty knowing "when to say when" with respect to drinking, leading to the infamous "hangover." By definition, a hangover refers to the negative physical and psychological effect that occur after drinking too much—the most common symptoms include headache, nausea, dizziness, sleepiness and even anxiety. According to the Mayo Clinic,[4] hangovers are caused by dehydration due to increased urination (light headedness), activation of the immune/inflammatory response (concentration/memory impairments) and blood vessel dilation (headaches). While there are some reported "hangover cures," none works better than abstaining from drinking! While the majority of hangovers subside within 24 hours of the drinking episode, it can feel like an eternity for the person experiencing it—it essentially feels like the 24-hour flu, only worse (see the figure "Hangover anatomy"). Unlike the 24-hour flu, drinking recklessly and to excess can lead to serious consequences (blackouts and alcohol poisoning).

---

4   www.mayoclinic.org/diseases-conditions/hangovers/basics/definition/con-20025464

Throat and mouth feel dry and scratchy because of dehydration.

Muscles become weak from dehydration and low blood-sugar levels.

Liver builds up fatty and lactic acids, impairing the body's ability to metabolize sugar. This results in low blood sugar, which can cause weakness and mood disturbances.

Stomach lining becomes inflamed, delaying digestion and excess gastric acid contributes to nausea.

Pancreas increases production of digestive chemicals causing pain, nausea and vomiting.

Brain's blood vessels dilate, causing a throbbing headache.

Pituitary gland releases improper amounts of several hormones, disrupting the brain's circadian rhythm and interfering with normal kidney functions.

Central nervous system becomes chemically overexcited causing sweating tremors and sensitivity to light, sound and touch.

Heart can become inflamed and start beating with an abnormal rhythm.

Kidneys fail to reabsorb water causing increased urination and dehydration.

Bladder can feel increased need for urination.

Hangover anatomy

It is Just One Drink...

Complicating matters is the fact that very few people actually *understand* the true definition of a single "drink." Young adults are known for using the customary "red Solo cup," which is *not* an accurate measure of one drink. This overconsumption likely contributes to the drinking issues prevalent among the young adult age group (see the figure "Measurements of alcohol intake"). Table 5.1 illustrates the effects of alcohol as a function of blood alcohol concentration and is a good source of education about the ways in which alcohol can impact behaviors, while Table 5.2 helps young adults understand the consequences of levels of drinking and the associated terms.

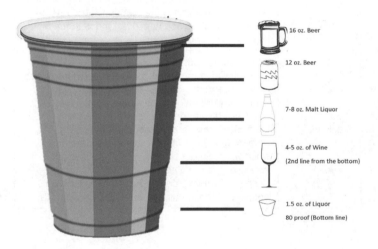

16 oz. Beer

12 oz. Beer

7-8 oz. Malt Liquor

4-5 oz. of Wine
(2nd line from the bottom)

1.5 oz. of Liquor
80 proof (Bottom line)

Measurements of alcohol intake—standard drink equivalents

Table 5.2 Drinking terms defined	
Intoxication (i.e., drunkenness)	Alcohol intoxication is defined as when the quantity of alcohol the person consumes produces behavioral or physical abnormalities. Alcohol is the generic term for ethanol. A person who is intoxicated with alcohol may have euphoria, poor coordination and movement, poor judgment, memory loss, slurred speech, confusion and even coma and death if the person consumes enough alcohol.[5]
Hangover	Severe headaches, nausea and other physiological symptoms that typically occur the morning after an evening of drinking (but not exclusively in the morning).
Alcohol poisoning	The sometimes fatal consequence of drinking large amounts of alcohol in a short period of time. Alcohol poisoning can affect your breathing, heart rate, body temperature and gag reflex and potentially lead to coma and death.
Blackout	When someone drinks in excess. Alcohol is considered a depressant, and when the dose is high enough, depressants are known to impair memory acquisition. When someone blacks out, it means that while they appear to be awake, alert and intoxicated, their brain is actually not making long-term memories of what's happening. Oftentimes, when you blackout while drinking, you are still able to engage in physical activities that can do harm (i.e., walking, driving, sexual behaviors, etc.) because of the impaired mental and physical state.

---

5   eMedicineHealth (2014)

Binge Drinking

About one in four teenagers and young adults will drink to excess—or binge drink.[6] As previously stated, BAC will vary with things like your height/weight and metabolism and the use of other medications, but generally speaking, "binge drinking occurs when males consume five or more drinks, and when females consume four or more drinks, in under two hours."[7] Binge drinking reportedly peaks near the age of 21, with less experienced drinkers ingesting higher volumes of alcohol more often—obviously a dangerous combination. Binge drinking occurs when you consume a large amount of alcohol in a short period of time, bringing your BAC to 0.08 grams or above. This sounds very technical, but simply stated, this is the point at which most people are too impaired to drive and when people are more likely to die from alcohol poisoning. Particularly for inexperienced drinkers, one drink can quickly turn into two or three or seven and lead to risky behaviors and/or medical crisis. It can be tempting to drink and be impulsive and carefree; however, there are serious consequences to these behaviors (see the figure "Risks of binge drinking").

---

6   CDC (2010)
7   National Institute on Alcohol Abuse and Alcoholism (2004)

RISKS OF BINGE DRINKING

- Vomiting (and hangover the next day).

- Blacking out/becoming unconscious (note: it is especially dangerous to vomit when you are passed out, as this could lead to choking).

- Getting alcohol poisoning (which can be lethal).

- Being involved in accidents or receiving unintentional injuries.

- Becoming a victim of sexual assault.

- Sustaining neurological damage.

Get Familiar with Alcohol in a Safe Setting

If you are interested in experimenting with alcohol you must consider safety concerns. If you are curious or interested in learning more about drinking, you might try starting at home, in a safe environment and under the care of someone who can be responsible. You will want to understand *what* to drink (e.g., only wine), the *volume* of the alcoholic beverages (e.g., 8 oz light beer), the alcohol *content*/proof and/or the *number* of drinks and the associated effects on your individual body.

You might prefer to "practice" drinking around trusted friends or family members where loved ones can monitor and process your reaction to it. Drinking for the first time in a stressful and unfamiliar setting with lots of sensory overstimulation and unfamiliar people can be disastrous.

Allowing for safe and monitored experimentation with alcohol at home or with trusted people may serve as a preview that can inform alcohol-related safety planning for the future.

The authors do not recommend that individuals with ASD engage in drinking or drug use. Most psychotropic medications come with a warning about alcohol/ medication interactions. As well, drinking can lead to increased vulnerability in an already vulnerable population.

Avoiding Peer Pressure—Drinking Responsibly

You may find that the pressure to drink is the most overwhelming part of your drinking concerns. Like many other young adults, you might not have any interest in drinking or not like the taste of alcohol. While stating outright that drinking "isn't your thing" can be great; it can also be very difficult. Instead, you can choose to avoid this pressure by using simple techniques like "always having a glass in your hand." Some of these tips really help when you wish to abstain from drinking and avoid peer pressure. Sometimes you simply want to enjoy one drink and make sure that you do not become impaired. Tip 5.1 provides guidance on how to avoid or control drinking when in a crowd.

TIP 5.1 Tips to avoid/control drinking

☑ Carry a non-alcoholic drink in your hand—add a small straw and a lime and it will look like an alcoholic drink (e.g., tonic water and lime).

☑ Order a non-alcoholic beer and pour it into a glass (remember, most non-alcoholic beers still have some alcohol content).

☑ Drink slowly—it is not a race.

☑ Alternate each alcoholic drink with a glass of water.

☑ Eat a healthy meal before drinking—don't drink on an empty stomach.

☑ Pay attention to your body—if you are feeling dizzy, walking funny, slurring your words, feeling nauseous, not acting like yourself, etc., stop drinking, have a glass of water and find a trusted friend.

Alcohol and Minors Don't Mix

If you are of legal age to drink, you should never provide alcohol to minors or purchase alcohol for minors, as you could be legally cited for contributing to the delinquency of a minor. A good rule of thumb is never to buy alcohol for anyone. Also, when hosting a party attended by minors who are drinking, regardless of whether or not the host bought the alcohol, you could face legal ramifications for any accidents or injuries sustained (see Tip 5.2). It is best to avoid having alcohol at parties that include a lot of underage people, especially if they are not close friends.

TIP 5.2 **Warning**[8]

All states prohibit providing alcohol to persons under 21, although states may have limited exceptions relating to lawful employment, religious activities, or consent by a parent, guardian, or spouse. Among states that have an exception related to such family member consent, that exception often is limited to specific locations (such as private locations, private residences, or in the parent or guardian's home.) No state has an exception that permits anyone other than a family member to provide alcohol to a minor on private property. In addition, many states have laws that provide that "social hosts" are responsible for underage drinking events on property they own, lease, or otherwise control, whether or not the social host actually provides the alcohol.

When Others Don't Follow the Rules

Due to the characteristics of autism spectrum disorders you might be a rigid rule follower, and you may want others to stick to the rules, as well. At times, you may feel it is your responsibility to "tattle" on friends who are drinking.

> I tend to see drinking in a very concrete legal terms. Like when I went into my friend's dorm room and saw her drinking a beer. I asked her if she was 21—which I knew she wasn't. I asked her how she got the beer. I eventually told the resident advisor (RA) that they were drinking because it is not permitted in the dorms and she

---

8   Federal Trade Commission (2015)

was underage. My friend definitely got mad at me, but I had to tell her because it was against the rules. (Marianna, young adult with ASD)

It is difficult to navigate the line between doing what is right and making sure others do it as well. It is important to remember that there are social consequences to "tattling" including isolation, bullying and other acts of retaliation. Sometimes it is better to tell an intermediary who can translate your message to the necessary authority, allowing you to save face[9] with your friends, but still address the problematic (or even illegal) behavior. In the example above, Marianna had enough insight to understand that her friend was mad at her for telling the RA and getting her in trouble, but she remained fixated on the violation of that law and had difficulty seeing the perspective of her friend who was engaging in underage drinking. While Marianna was correct regarding the legality of the issue, she violated the social norm of "telling" on a friend.

Keeping Drinks Safe

The use of drugs like Rohypnol or Xanax to spike drinks is a very serious problem in public places (e.g., bars, clubs) and particularly for young adults. When someone spikes a drink, they put a drug, usually one that cannot be detected visually or by taste, into the drink, which impairs an individual's functioning. The motivation for this act is usually to lower the inhibitions of the individual such that the person who

---

9 "Saving face" is the desire to avoid humiliation or embarrassment, maintain dignity or preserve reputation. In this particular instance, it means that you would not have to be embarrassed or fearful of "telling" because you would not be identified as the person who "told."

spiked the drink can engage in sexual relations with the drugged person or rob them of their money or possessions. Because the individual who receives the drug is impaired and unable to make decisions or give consent, any sexual acts while under the influence of this drug would be considered rape. This is why drugs like Rohypnol, Klonopin, Xanax, GHB and ketamine are often referred to as "date rape drugs."

Research suggests that, "with no official statistics and a culture that makes victims feel there's no point in telling anyone, drink spiking is going largely unchecked."[10] Safeguards to avoid drink spiking should be implemented and you should always use the buddy system when drinking in a public setting (see Tip 5.3). If someone starts to feel funny (e.g., sick, dizzy, lightheaded, intense fatigue, etc.) after ingesting a drink, you should notify a friend or authority figure right away so they can act fast (see the following section).

TIP 5.3 Safeguards to avoid drink spiking

- ☑ Never leave your drink unattended.
- ☑ Do not accept drinks from people you do not know or have only just met.
- ☑ Watch the bartender prepare your drink and look out for any suspicious behavior/tampering with your drink.
- ☑ If possible, stick with bottled drinks.
- ☑ Pay attention to how you are feeling. Drugs that are commonly used for drink spiking cause lightheadedness, blurry vision and lowered inhibitions. It is unlikely that

10 Young-Powell (2014)

you would be able to see, smell or taste the presence of these drugs.

Sound the Alarms

Newer technology has made staying safe a bit easier. Designed for women in particular, the Safelet bracelet allows the wearer to signal for help if they feel unsafe. The bracelet works via Bluetooth and an app on the wearer's phone to alert others (friends, family or other designated loved ones and the police) to their exact location. Also, the bracelet immediately begins an audio recording when the alarm button is pressed—the audio is concurrently transmitted to the police.[11] Other watches and bands that are more gender neutral are also available. Additionally there are phone apps with geotracking services and ways to alert friends or family members (and local emergency services) that you are in need of assistance (i.e., Circle of 6, Guardly, bSafe).

Drinking and Driving
CAUTIONS IN THE CAR

When considering going to a party or pub, transportation is a key safety concern. It is important to set clear boundaries in advance of the situation and to have planned backup if needed in case a friend or "ride" (the person who is transporting you to and from the party) has been drinking. In these instances it is essential to find an alternate mode of transportation. A general rule of thumb is never to get into a car with anyone who has been drinking.

---

11 More information about this line can be found at www.safelet.com; prices range from $79 to $129.

Not only is drinking and driving illegal, it is also extremely dangerous and life threatening to the driver, the passengers and the public at large. Traffic accidents are the leading cause of death among teens and young adults, and more than half of driving fatalities for drivers aged 21–24 involve alcohol.[12] Therefore, finding a safe and reliable ride to and from the social event is critical and advanced planning is necessary. Again, you should avoid getting into a car with anyone who has been drinking. If everyone in the group has been drinking, using public transportation or calling a taxi/car service are the best options. It is important to have a zero-tolerance "policy" on this issue and never ride in a car if the driver has had any alcohol. If you are interested in experimenting with alcohol, you must have a good understanding of the dangers of driving under the influence and have the skills necessary to navigate public transportation or taxis/car services.

DESIGNATED DRIVER—THE "DD"

For years, young adults have been using a system of shared responsibility to ensure safety when drinking outside of the home by taking turns acting as the designated driver or DD. This person is charged with abstaining from alcohol at the event to ensure a safe ride home for their friends. While this is a saf*er* choice for young adults who will be drinking, it is difficult to control other people and their choices to drink and drive. If at all possible it is best to leave the party early and be off the roads before midnight.

One other common issue involves ensuring the safety of other people and making sure they do not drink and drive, for example, if the designated driver decided to have "just one drink," but is acting a little funny (e.g., slurring their

---

12 National Highway Traffic Safety Administration (2004)

words, walking unsteadily), it can be difficult to address this issue, especially if they insist that they are "fine" and insist on driving. In these cases it is important that you trust your instincts, prioritize your safety and find an alternative method of transportation (see the "Driver Please" section). It is difficult to know if people are sober enough to drive by simply looking at them. Also, even though a person might plan not to drink or to have only a "few drinks," some people change their mind while out socializing and drink more than they intend. Additionally, people sometimes feel braver or invincible when drinking, so they are inclined to say, "I'm OK to drive" when in fact they may not be fine at all. This can leave you stuck in an unsafe or unclear situation. These situations also require awkward but necessary conversations that are especially difficult to navigate (see Social Script 5.2).

SOCIAL SCRIPT 5.2 NEGOTIATING THE RIDE HOME

In the situation below the designated driver decides to drink, placing their friends in an awkward position. The script highlights how someone might check in with a friend about their drinking and offer to drive.

Taylor: "You ready to go?"

Michele: "Sure, just let me finish my drink."

Taylor: "I thought you weren't drinking. How many drinks have you had?"

Michele: "I don't know. Two or three beers... I'm fine."

Taylor: "Why don't I drive? Better to be safe than sorry."

While it is responsible to offer friends a safe ride and try and keep them off the road, you cannot always control the behavior of others. People who have been drinking are often not aware of their impairment, have clouded judgment and do not recognize their physical strength. It is important to communicate the legalities of driving drunk and to offer them a safe ride and if possible, take their keys (see Social Script 5.3).

SOCIAL SCRIPT 5.3 CONTINUED NEGOTIATIONS

In this case, the passenger is still negotiating the ride home (when someone who has been drinking plans to get behind the wheel). It often takes more than one attempt to get someone to recognize that they shouldn't be driving. See the continued conversation below between Michele and Taylor.

Michele: "Taylor, I'm fine—let me drive."

Taylor: "I'm not comfortable with you driving—I am going to find another ride. Are you sure you don't want me to drive?"

Michele: "Dude, let me drive! It's not a big deal."

Taylor: "You should not drive—it's not worth it—you could hurt yourself or someone else. Give me your keys."

DRIVER, PLEASE! USING APPS TO ACCESS SAFE TRANSPORTATION

As mentioned above, if all of the individuals in a group have been drinking, it is in everyone's best interest to look for alternative modes of transportation. Options include public transportation, taxis and newer driving services (usually restricted to larger cities) like Uber or Lyft. One way to ensure easy access to these services is to preload the contact numbers for the respective transportation modes into your phone or download the apps on your smartphone. As well, most public transport routes have an app that tells you exactly when the next bus or train is coming. Apps like Uber and Lyft summon drivers who are in your immediate area and let you know approximately how long it will be before pickup (see Tip 5.4). These apps make it easy to track your ride and communicate with the driver at the touch of a button (no talking necessary!). You can also enter your destination in advance so that the driver arrives ready to get you home safely.

TIP 5.4 Transportation considerations

☑ Have a safe ride planned to and from the event. Calling a taxi or using public transportation for the first time after a night out socializing is not the best decision. Practice how to use them with a friend or family member on several occasions during several times of the day or days of the week to help generalize the skills.

☑ Driving yourself: If you are not drinking and plan to drive, ensure you are taking a safe vehicle, with sufficient gas.

☑ Getting rides from friends: Do not get into a car with anyone who has been drinking or using illegal substances.

☑ Public transportation: If you are using public transportation or a car service, be sure to practice how to use these services successfully.

☑ Taxis/Uber: Preprogram numbers for cab/driving companies into your phone.

☑ Know the social protocol for use of cabs and taxis (e.g., how to hail a cab, call a cab, what to do if your cab does not show up, what to do if your cab/car is taken by another group of people, how to pay/tip, etc.).

☑ Be able to discern a legitimate cab from one that is less reputable.

☑ Discuss how much a ride in a cab is likely to cost.

☑ Be aware that people often change locations and plans impulsively—think about how you want to handle that. If you do change locations, be sure to notify friends or family.

☑ You should also be aware that sometimes people "bar-hop" (go from one bar to another bar) and you need to decide in advance how you plan to address these possible location changes.

Using the Buddy System

Alcohol can make you act differently than normal (e.g., more flirtatious, more aggressive, less inhibited), especially if you are not accustomed to drinking or are drinking a different kind of alcohol. When under the influence of drugs or alcohol, you are more likely to engage in behaviors that can compromise your safety or the safety of others (e.g., risky sexual behaviors, fighting, driving while intoxicated). For this reason, it is highly recommend that if you have plans to drink alcohol, especially at a pub, club or party, you bring along a trusted friend who serves as the "buddy" or social interpreter (if needed) and as a source of safety and support. In turn, you also need to watch over your buddy by checking in regularly with him/her to ensure they are making good decisions and are also safe (see Tip 5.5).

A Bad Mix: Medications and Alcohol/ Recreational Drugs

While the largest concern among parents with respect to drug use is recreational drugs (e.g., marijuana, heroin, etc.), it is important that drug/alcohol education begins with a conversation about safety considerations with respect to prescription medications. More than half of individuals on the autism spectrum (approximately 65%) have a prescription for a psychotropic medication.[13] With a host of psychiatric comorbidities (e.g., attention deficit hyperactivity disorder (ADHD), anxiety and depression) and medical complexities (e.g., epilepsy, gastrointestinal problems and metabolic challenges), the likelihood that you will be on a prescribed medication at some point throughout your teen and young adult years is very high. Therefore, any conversation about parties, and drinking, must include a conversation about medication interactions.

Research on drug interactions, particularly between prescription drugs and recreational drugs, is very limited. There are seemingly endless combinations of prescription and recreational drugs of which many interactions remain dangerously unknown. It is often the case that negative and even lethal interactions are discovered after someone has had a negative reaction.

13 Spencer *et al.* (2013)

TIP 5.5 Guidelines for responsible drinking behaviors

☑ Do not mix prescription drugs and alcohol and check with a health professional before deciding to drink.

☑ If you do not want to drink it, say no; do not act on pressures to drink.

☑ People often try to pressure others to drink when they are drinking. **Just say no** and only drink what is comfortable and safe for you.

☑ Similarly, do not act on pressures to buy alcohol for minors; one of the young adults we spoke to mentioned being pressured by her younger brother to buy him alcohol. The consequences of buying alcohol for a minor can include fines and even jail time.

☑ The amount of food you have eaten impacts intoxication level; drinking when you have not eaten is especially troublesome.

☑ Sip your drink, do not gulp.

☑ Always have a designated driver and/or a buddy (someone who is not drinking) to watch out for you when you are drinking.

☑ Drink things that you are familiar with and are pre-prepared (e.g. a bottle of beer or glass of a specific type of wine you have tried before); there is a lot of variability between bartenders and establishments about how much alcohol is in one drink.

☑ Read labels for the amount of alcohol by volume or ask the bartender if you are unsure.

☑ Beware of alcohol/liquor in other forms (e.g., Jell-O shots, alcohol infused fruit, etc.).

☑ Be aware of your family history; if alcoholism and drug addiction run in your family, it is not recommended that you experiment with these substances because you are at greater risk for abuse/addiction.

Drugs
Recreational Drug Use

> I did have some friends who started on that road (i.e., doing drugs), but drugs never appealed to me because I saw friends squander opportunities and go from using drugs to selling drugs to significant legal problems. It also helps me to visualize the consequences of drug use and really reminds me to avoid them. Also, in the case of drugs, I see my anxiety as a blessing in disguise—I am afraid of drugs and the consequences so I avoid them. (Patrick, young adult with ASD)

The most widely used recreational drug among the young adult population is marijuana. The popularity of marijuana is increasing, particularly with its legalization in several states. According to the National Institute on Drug Abuse, in 2013 36 percent of college students said they used marijuana in the past year, compared with 30 percent in 2006. Interestingly, young adults not in college were twice as likely to smoke marijuana daily compared with the college group.[14] When a young adult is not engaged in meaningful academic or

---

14 National Institute on Drug Abuse (2013)

occupational activities, they may be more at risk for drug usage. It was also suggested that rates of marijuana use in the young adult age group are higher than they have been in over three decades.[15] While usage is quite commonplace, it is still critical to remember that it is illegal in most states and being caught using or in possession of an illegal substance is likely to have serious repercussions.

One special concern with marijuana is the possibility of ingesting the drug in other forms like "edibles" (e.g., brownies, candies, chocolate infused with marijuana). Like the prior discussion of alcohol, it is important to be cautious about what you eat or drink in a party atmosphere. With marijuana being legalized in some US states, the drug is likely to become even more prevalent. While making a conscious decision to smoke marijuana is a more voluntary decision, with the popularity of "edible" marijuana, it may be easy for you to be unaware that you are ingesting the substance. While not a critical public health concern at present, the rates of children accidentally ingesting marijuana has increased in recent years.[16] You may be more naïve or vulnerable, so it is important to be aware that drugs can be infused into everyday edibles, like brownies, cookies or candies.

Finally, it is important to be aware of trends related to other drugs. Prescription drugs are often abused. Some medications (frequently prescribed to young adults with autism) are attractive to "friends" who want to steal and/or abuse their medications. Stimulant medications including Adderall, Ritalin and Strattera are frequently sought on the black market. Abuse of prescription drugs is highest among young adults aged 18–25, with 5.9 percent reporting nonmedical

---

15 National Institute on Drug Abuse (2013)
16 Monte, Zane and Heard (2015)

use in the past month while rates of other illicit drugs have remained stable over the past several years and even decades. However, it is critical to know the facts.[17] Drug abuse across all categories is highest among young adults and teens, with nearly one in four reporting illegal drug use in the past month according to the National Institute on Drug Abuse.

It is important to have some background on illegal drugs, familiarizing yourself with the formal and "street" names for the drugs and being aware of what the drugs look like and the formats different drugs may be in.

Summary

Drinking and drug use are critical topics requiring serious education, awareness and planning. If you experience comorbid medical/psychiatric conditions, and take medication for these issues, drug interactions are a very real concern. Experimentation with drugs or alcohol should not be attempted. If you are curious or interested in trying alcohol or drugs, we caution you to pay close attention to the aforementioned tips, strategies and considerations to ensure your personal safety and the safety of those around you. Again, while you may decide to abstain from alcohol and/or drugs, that will not prevent others from using them. Education is a great tool for staying safe; being educated about drug and alcohol use will help you safely navigate the world around you.

---

17 NIDA (2014)

References

Center for Disease Control (2010) Fact-sheets underage drinking. Available from www.cdc.gov/alcohol/fact-sheets/underage-drinking.htm, accessed on 4 February 2016.

Centers for Disease Control (2015) *Effects of Blood Alcohol Concentration (BAC)*. Atlanta, GA: Centers for Disease Control. Available at www.cdc.gov/Motorvehiclesafety/impaired_driving/bac.html, accessed 1 November 2015.

eMedicineHealth (2014) *Alcohol Intoxication Definition*. New York: WebMD. Available at: www.emedicinehealth.com/alcohol_intoxication/article_em.htm#alcohol_intoxication_definition, accessed on 1 November 2015.

Federal Trade Commission (2015) *Alcohol Laws by State*. Washington, DC: Federal Trade Commission. Available at www.consumer.ftc.gov/articles/0388-alcohol-laws-state, accessed on 31 October 2015.

Monte, A. A., Zane, R. D. and Heard, K. J. (2015) 'The implications of marijuana legalization in Colorado.' *JAMA 313*, 3, 241–242.

Naimi, T. S., Brewer, R. D., Mokdad, A., Denny, C., Serdula, M. K. and Marks, J. S. (2003) 'Binge drinking among US adults.' *JAMA 289*, 1, 70–75.

National Highway Traffic Safety Administration (NHTSA) (2004) *Traffic Safety Facts 2003 Annual Report: Early Edition*. Washington, DC: US Dept. of Transportation.

National Institute on Alcohol Abuse and Alcoholism (2004) 'NIAAA council approves definition of binge drinking.' *NIAAA Newsletter 3*, 3.

National Institute on Alcohol Abuse and Alcoholism (2014) *Harmful Interactions*. Bethesda, MD: National Institute on Alcohol Abuse and Alcoholism. Available at http://pubs.niaaa.nih.gov/publications/Medicine/medicine.htm, accessed on 1 November 2015.

National Institute on Drug Abuse (2014) *DrugFacts: Nationwide Trends*. Available at www.drugabuse.gov/national-survey-drug-use-health, accessed on 1 November 2015.

Spencer, D., Marshall, J., Post, B., Kulakodlu, M., *et al.* (2013) 'Psychotropic medication use and polypharmacy in children with autism spectrum disorders.' *Pediatrics 132*, 5, 833–840.

Substance Abuse and Mental Health Services Administration (2013) *Results from the 2012 National Survey on Drug Use and Health: Summary of National Findings* (NSDUH Series H-46, HHS Publication No. SMA 13-4795). Rockville, MD: Substance Abuse and Mental Health Services Administration.

Young-Powell, A. (2014) 'Drink spiking: Victims don't report and the crime goes unpunished.' *The Guardian*, 23 August 2014. Available at www.theguardian.com/education/2014/aug/23/drink-spiking-victims-dont-report-crime-unpunished, accessed on 31 October 2015.

Appendix 5.1

Commonly Used Medicines for ASD that Interact With Alcohol[1]

Symptom/ disorders	Medication (brand name)	Medication (generic name)	Some possible reactions with alcohol
Anxiety and epilepsy	Ativan®	Lorazepam	Drowsiness, dizziness; increased risk for overdose; slowed or difficulty breathing; impaired motor control; unusual behavior; memory problems
	BuSpar®	Buspirone	
	Klonopin®	Clonazepam	
	Librium®	Chlordiazepoxide	
	Paxil®	Paroxetine	
	Valium®	Diazepam	
	Xanax®	Alprazolam	
	Herbal preparations (Kava Kava)		Liver damage, drowsiness
	Naprosyn®	Naproxen	
	Voltaren®	Diclofenac	

1 National Institute on Alcohol Abuse and Alcoholism (2014)

Attention and concentration (attention deficit/ hyperactivity disorder)	Adderall®	Amphetamine/dextro-amphetamine	Dizziness, drowsiness, impaired concentration (methylphenidate, dexmethylphenidate); possible increased risk for heart problems (amphetamine, dextroamphetamine, lisdexamfetamine); liver damage (atomoxetine)
	Concerta®, Ritalin®	Methylphenidate	
	Dexedrine®	Dextroamphetamine	
	Focalin®	Dexmethylphenidate	
	Strattera®	Atomoxetine	
	Vyvanse®	Lisdexamfetamine	

Cont.

Symptom/ disorders	Medication (brand name)	Medication (generic name)	Some possible reactions with alcohol
	Abilify®	Aripriprazone	Drowsiness, dizziness; increased risk for overdose; increased feelings of depression or hopelessness (all medications); impaired motor control (quetiapine, mirtazapine; increased alcohol effect (bupropion); liver damage (duloxetine)

Monoamine oxidase inhibitors (MAOIs), such as tranylcypromine and phenelzine, when combined with alcohol, may result in serious heart-related side effects. Risk for dangerously high blood pressure is increased when MAOIs are mixed with tyramine, a byproduct found in beer and red wine |
	Anafranil®	Clomipramine	
	Celexa®	Citalopram	
	Clozaril®	Clozapine	
	Cymbalta®	Duloxetine	
	Desyrel®	Trazodone	
	Effexor®	Venlafaxine	
Depression	Elavil®	Amitriptyline	
	Geodon®	Ziprasidone	
	Invega®	Paliperidone	
	Lexapro®	Escitalopram	
	Luvox®	Fluvoxamine	
	Nardil®	Phenelzine	
	Norpramin®	Desipramine	
	Pamate®	Tranylcypromine	

Depression	Paxil®	Paroxetine
	Pristiq®	Desevenlafaxine
	Prozac®	Fluoxetine
	Remeron®	Mirtazapine
	Risperdal®	Risperidone
	Seroquel®	Quetiapine
	Serzone®	Nefazodone
	Symbyax®	Fluoxetine/ Olanzapine
	Wellbutrin®	Bupropion
	Zoloft®	Sertraline
	Zyprexa®	Olanzapine
	Herbal preparations (St. John's Wort)	
	Zocor®	Simvastatin

Drowsiness, dizziness; increased risk for overdose; increased feelings of depression or hopelessness (all medications); impaired motor control (quetiapine, mirtazapine); increased alcohol effect (bupropion); liver damage (duloxetine)

Monoamine oxidase inhibitors (MAOIs), such as tranylcypromine and phenelzine, when combined with alcohol, may result in serious heart-related side effects. Risk for dangerously high blood pressure is increased when MAOIs are mixed with tyramine, a byproduct found in beer and red wine

Cont.

Symptom/ disorders	Medication (brand name)	Medication (generic name)	Some possible reactions with alcohol
Infections	Acrodantin®	Nitrofurantoin	Fast heartbeat, sudden changes in blood pressure; stomach pain, upset stomach, vomiting, headache or flushing or redness of the face; liver damage (isoniazid, ketoconazole)
	Flagyl®	Metronidazole	
	Grisactin®	Griseofulvin	
	Nizoral®	Ketoconazole	
	Nydrazid®	Isoniazid	
	Seromycin®	Cycloserine	
	Tindamax®	Tinidazole	
	Zithromax®	Azithromycin	
Mood stabilizers	Depakene®, Depakote®	Valproic acid	Drowsiness, dizziness; tremors; increased risk for side effects, such as restlessness, impaired motor control; loss of appetite; stomach upset; irregular bowel movement; joint or muscle pain; depression; liver damage (valproic acid)
	Eskalith®, Eskalith®CR, Lithobid	Lithium	
	Soma®	Carisoprodol	

Sleep problems	Ambien®	Zolpidem	Increased drowsiness
	Lunesta™	Eszopiclone	
	Prosom™	Estazolam	
	Restoril®	Temazepam	
	Sominex®	Diphenhydramine	
	Unisom®	Doxylamine	
	Herbal preparations (chamomile, valerian, lavender)		Increased drowsiness

Chapter 6

Stressing Out

Managing Stress and Health

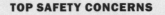

TOP SAFETY CONCERNS

★ Medical conditions.

★ Medication management and storage.

★ Mental health.

★ Treatment adherence.

★ Emotion regulation and stress.

★ Challenges to healthy eating.

★ Sleep concerns.

★ Physical fitness.

It can be really hard to deal with everything that I have going on. In addition to the autism, I also have seizures and severe anxiety. Luckily, I have good support from my family and a really great team of professionals who have helped me find the right medications and treatments. There was a time when nothing seemed to be going right and I was really anxious and depressed. My family would not let me give up and eventually I started finding things that worked for me. My advice to others is to stay positive and hopeful. There may be challenges and times when I don't feel like going to therapy or taking my meds, but mostly, I follow "doctor's orders" and it usually helps me feel better and do the things I want to accomplish. I have also benefitted from eating healthier and working out—relieving my stress was a big part of controlling my anxiety. (Anonymous, young adult with ASD)

The social challenges associated with autism can make navigating daily life a bit more complicated and stressful for you. When paired with another medical or psychiatric condition, ASD becomes more complicated, potentially compromising your ability to cope in a high-stress situation and remain calm and safe. Coping mechanisms that work for you in private settings (e.g., pacing, swinging, stimming, positive self-talk, etc.), are often discouraged in public, exacerbating or escalating existing health issues (psychological, medical, physical). This chapter focuses on prevention and management of safety issues that are related to your psychological, medical and physical health including: medication management, treatment teams, emotion regulation, sleep habits, healthy eating and hygiene.

Medical Comorbidities

As an individual with autism you likely have a higher than expected chance of having other medical conditions, including: eczema, allergies, asthma, ear and respiratory infections, gastrointestinal problems, severe headaches, migraines and seizures.[1] Simply having the common cold can

---

1   Kohane *et al.* (2012)

make everyday tasks more difficult and reduce coping skills for everyone. For you, having a chronic medical condition can substantially interfere with coping strategies, quality of life and management of daily living. Unlike the common cold, ASD does not go away with time and chicken soup. Therefore, it is important to implement strategies that maximize safety and support your effective coping skills. It "takes a village"— the best results occur when psychologists, psychiatrists, physicians, therapists, allies, friends, family and other team members work together to support you.

Managing Medical Needs

An awareness of your personal medical information is the first step to managing your medical needs. You will need to know your personal health history (and even family history) in the event of a medical emergency. Collecting, organizing and storing this information allows for quick reference at doctors' appointments or when completing paperwork. It can be very helpful to create a medical history card. This is a simple, yet effective way to keep track of important medical information and ensure accuracy when communicating with health professionals. For example, say you are taken to the emergency room for a broken wrist. The medical team will ask a lot of questions about your medical history and current medications. If you are in distress (or pain) you might have a hard time remembering or communicating this personal information, especially in an overwhelming environment like the emergency room or walk-in clinic. The medical history card can be shared with the provider or team, ensuring that information is reported in an accurate manner. The medical history card should be stored in your wallet or purse, preferably next to your medical insurance card so that it is readily accessible. The "card" could also be stored electronically in your smartphone, alongside copies of your insurance card, identification and other important documents. It is critical that the card be regularly reviewed and updated to ensure accuracy, especially around your medications, dosages and allergies (see the figure "Medical history card"). The following information should be contained in the card:

- Diagnoses: if possible, list complete diagnostic information (including ASD).

- Medications: names, dosages and directions.

- Prior surgeries.

- Allergies.

- Miscellaneous—contacts, pacemaker, dental implant, etc.

- Physician's names and contact information.

- Insurance information: with insured's name, group number and phone number.

- Emergency contact: have a list of two or three individuals who should be contacted and how to contact them; it is wise to have more than one individual in case someone does not answer their phone.

- Family medical history.

<u>Medical History Card</u>

Name: Emily Marie Taylor   **Date of Birth:** 10/28/1992

Diagnoses:

• Autism Spectrum Disorder (previously known as Asperger's)

• Attention Deficit Hyperactive Disorder (ADHD)

Medications:

• Vyvanse 30 mg (orange and white capsules) Take in the morning with a light snack.

• Risperdal 2 mg (round orange tablet) Take every night before bed.

Prior surgeries: None   **Miscellaneous:** I wear contacts.

Allergies: None, but dietary retrictions (gluten free)

Physician's Name: Anne Hurst, MD   **Contact:** 423-855-3111

Insurance Information:

Policy holder: Tracy Taylor (mother)

Group number: 000252650140

Emergency Contact:

Tracy Taylor (mother): 423-809-2524

Chad Taylor (father): 415-706-8975

Family Medical History: High blood pressure (paternal grandfather), breast cancer (maternal grandmother), diabetes (father)

Medical history card

If you have a life-threatening condition, a condition that might render you unconscious (i.e., seizure, severe allergy, diabetes) or causes you to have significant challenges with communication, having a medical alert system or device may be beneficial. A medical alert device can include an engraved bracelet with relevant diagnostic information or a more technologically advanced system like an alarm that can alert medical professionals in the event of an emergency. For example, if you have diabetes you could pass out as a result of very low blood sugar; if you were wearing a medical alert bracelet or pendant, bystanders and professionals could more quickly identify the medical issue.

Patient-focused Care

In addition to communicating with outside health experts in the event of an emergency, you must also have the skills necessary to self-advocate among your healthcare team. Understanding your medical history, communicating health-related needs and being an active participant in your healthcare is a prerequisite to navigating independent living safely. People may falsely believe that they have to continue to make decisions regarding your health well into adulthood. Your family members are used to advocating on your behalf and professionals are also used to making assumptions about people with disabilities like ASD (e.g., individuals with autism often do not communicate well or may be uncomfortable with questions about their health). Given this, your opinion may be overlooked or assumed without clarification. Social Script 6.1 demonstrates a respectful and assertive way to communicate your need to be part of the team.

Note: Know your rights! When an individual is 18 or older (and not under guardianship of parents or another individual), they have the legal authority to make decisions about their own medical care. While many young adults with ASD welcome a trusted family member to attend some health-related appointments with them, it is for the individual to decide who attends appointments and who has access to their medical records and agree/disagree with the treatment plan.

SOCIAL SCRIPT 6.1 BECOMING PART OF THE TEAM

At the neurologist, Jennifer, a 25-year-old with ASD, is accompanied by her mother, Sandy. When discussing the use of a new medication to control her seizures, the neurologist is only talking to Mom and has left Jennifer out of the conversation.

Jennifer: "It appears that you are having a conversation about my medications without including me. I prefer that you discuss these issues with me, as I am directly impacted by the decisions and have valid opinions about my health and treatment."

Mom/Sandy: "OK. I am glad you said that. Do you want me to leave the room so you can talk with the doctor alone?"

Jennifer: "No, I would like your continued support I just don't want you to talk about me as if I am not here. I have a few questions about the side effects of this new medication I want to better understand."

Medications

Medications are often used to treat symptoms or secondary issues related to ASD (anxiety, depression, obsessive–compulsive disorder (OCD))—making medication management a part of your everyday life. Part of independent living includes managing medications safely. Gaining independence with medications/interventions requires a broad array of skills and strategies (see Tip 6.1).

TIP 6.1 Skills needed for independent medication management

Awareness of medications:

☑ Knowing name of medication (generic and brand name).

☑ Knowing medication dosage and frequency.

☑ Understanding the function/use of medication.

☑ Familiarity of side effects and how to self-evaluate these side effects.

☑ Understanding contraindications (e.g., do not take this medication on an empty stomach).

☑ Knowing potential interactions.

Medication monitoring:

☑ Medication and symptom monitoring is especially important when starting a new medication or when medications do not seem to be optimized. For example, with medications used to address symptoms of anxiety and/or depression, taking the time to regularly rate symptoms, feelings, side effects, etc. over a sufficient period time of time is important.

Access:

☑ Knowing how to attain the medications is essential (e.g., through going to the pharmacy in person, ordering the medications online, managing refills, what to do when you have run out of refills).

Finances:

☑ Being able to pay for medications and knowing how to communicate with insurance companies.

Communication and collaboration with medical team:

☑ While it is tempting for the prescribing physician to want to discuss medication only with the caregiver, it is crucial for you to be included in the conversation (and to advocate for yourself to be part of the conversation).

Remembering Medication

> I have been attempting to promote medication independence for Hikarih by giving her the responsibility to refill her own prescriptions. Medications were cheaper when they were filled via mail order and therefore had to be ordered in advance. Once, Hikarih forgot to refill her medications in a timely manner, and ran out before she was able to order them. We had to refill them in the pharmacy in person for an additional cost. Hikarih had to pay for it since it was her mistake for not ordering her medications on time. (Mother of young adult with ASD)

As an adult, you will have many commitments and distractions that compete for your attention every day, but it is important that you take special care to manage and monitor your medication. Useful strategies may include:

- scheduling regular pharmacy visits to ensure ongoing prescriptions are filled on time
- setting alarms on a watch or cell phone to remember to take or order medication
- organizing weekly and daily medications in a pillbox, pre-packaged pill packets or automatic pill dispenser.

There are multiple options for managing and remembering medication, so the goal is to find the option that works best and stick with it! Also, as mentioned above in the quote from Hikarih's mother, independent management of medications does not often happen without preparation, strategies and/or even incentives. As well, it's important to know your medications well to avoid any errors or accidental overdosing if given the wrong dose. Using one pharmacy consistently will greatly reduce the likelihood of errors, as will getting to know the pharmacists personally.

> Developing a trusting relationship with the pharmacist is critical. Because I feel comfortable asking her questions about interactions and side effects, it is safer. She is friendly and we are on a first-name basis. It also helps me feel less anxious about my medications because I feel like she knows me and won't make mistakes because she knows my history and stuff. It took a while for me to get comfortable, but it is worth it. (Patrick, young adult with ASD)

In the above quote, Patrick highlights the importance of establishing a relationship with the pharmacist. Because he knows his pharmacist well, he is comfortable asking her questions, which can support medication compliance. While Patrick has also benefited from the use of a pre-packaged pills service for his medications, he cautions that he once found that they put the wrong drug in the packet by mistake. You should be able to identify your medications by shape, color, size and markings. It was Patrick who caught the mistake in his medication, and now he regularly checks the package. If you have any questions or concerns about medications you should speak to the prescribing professional and/or the pharmacist immediately (see Tip 6.2).

TIP 6.2 Medication reminders and management

☑ Using a phone reminder (setting an alarm on the phone).

☑ Using visual reminders (e.g., a note on the refrigerator or coffee maker).

☑ Using a pillbox/organizer—a weekly or monthly pill organizer can help maintain medication safety. With a pill organizer, you put all of the pills you need to take each day in the slot corresponding to the day/date. This can serve as a reminder to take medications, prevent taking more than one pill (if you have difficulty remembering) and even save time by prepping the medications ahead of time.

☑ Pairing taking medication with something you have an easy time remembering to do can help it become a habit (i.e., take your medication right after you brush your teeth).

☑ When adding a new medication to the mix, allow yourself a few days to adjust and try medication over a weekend or at a time when you don't have other commitments.

☑ Using prepackaged medication services (i.e., medications are prepped in advance and packaged together by the pharmacy or service).

☑ While prepackaged medication services can be very helpful, it is still important to review the medications because mistakes can be made.

☑ Any pills that suddenly change in color/shape should not be taken; instead return medication to the pharmacy to inquire about the change. (It could be a generic version of the same pill or a different dosage.)

Non-compliance

The biggest problem is non-compliance. Once on the medication they feel like they do not need it. It's a cycle, institution-medication-non-compliance-institution. While many providers are great and are wonderful about talking to clients about the need to continually take medication and follow guidelines, so many young adults do not consistently take their meds or follow recommendations. If the problem is forgetting to take the medication, I typically suggest using products designed to help remind the elderly to take their medication (e.g., auto pill dispensers, large pillboxes, pill reminder apps, etc). (Beth Thompson, Milestones Autism Resources Teen/Adult Services Manager, social worker with specialization in young adults with ASD)

Adhere to Medication and Professional Recommendations

Medications, therapy and advice from professionals are useless unless they are followed as directed. If you have concerns or reservations about taking a medication or following the recommendation of a professional, it is highly recommended that you discuss these concerns with the professional rather than stopping (or not starting) the medication/intervention. In fact, abruptly stopping a medication is especially dangerous. There may be methods for a safe tapering of medication use, but all changes to medication should be done under the supervision of a healthcare profession.

- **Do**: Discuss treatment concerns with your health professional.

- **Don't**: Be secretive about your decisions related to your health and treatments.

Forgetting Medication: Consequences

Forgetting to take prescriptions, or otherwise not recognizing the necessity of medications, can have a negative impact on your emotional and physical well-being. When you don't take medication as prescribed, you or those around you might start to notice differences in your emotions and behaviors. This can lead to a medication spiral, during which you could have symptom exacerbation and even demonstrate erratic behavior.[2] Quality of life can quickly decline (e.g., work problems, relationship conflicts and trouble at home/work/ school) after only a few days of impaired concentration or depressed mood. Conversely, when you *do* take medicine as prescribed, the odds of feeling better and functioning better are much higher.

Remembering medication can be tough. In the book, *Expect a Miracle: A Mother/Son Asperger Journey of Determination and Triumph*, the author talks about how she and her son worked with medication management when he moved from the home into independent living:

> David had been taking his medication independently for years, but he occasionally needed reminders if his normal routine was altered. Seeking a way to distinguish

---

2 Rigler, Rutherford and Quinn (2015)

between meds, which were needed versus already taken, we utilized a partitioned pill-box. Dave prepared and replenished its contents weekly on a set day, and we began this practice prior to school's start to firmly establish the habit. Fortunately, these medications were timed to coincide with waking and bedtime personal needs, so linked to other tasks, they were rarely forgotten.[3]

Safely Storing Medications

It is important for young adults to maintain medications in a safe and secure location. Because many of the medications prescribed for individuals on the spectrum are also used recreationally and/or sold for profit on the streets, they are targets for theft and misuse. For example, stimulant medications used to treat ADHD are often stolen and then sold to individuals who do not need them.[4] Keeping medications and pillboxes stored in a lock box or safe is a simple way to ensure medication is safety out of the reach of others. The lock box/safe combination should always be kept confidential. Similarly, if a key is used to open the lock box/safe it should be stored in a location that is safe from others.

Psychological Comorbidities

The stress of having ASD combined with a medical/psychological complication is challenging and can negatively influence stress management and overall health (see Table 6.1). Approximately 75 percent of youth with ASD have a diagnosable mental health disorder alongside their autism diagnosis (i.e., depression, anxiety, ADHD), with anxiety

---

3   Petrovic and Petrovic (2014)
4   Rigler, Rutherford and Quinn (2015)

being the most common.[5] If you are experiencing any of the psychological symptoms mentioned above, it is important to consult with both mental health *and* medical professionals.

Note: Sometimes symptoms of depression or anxiety, for example, may have a medically related cause (i.e., hypothyroidism symptoms can mimic symptoms of depression). It is best to evaluate the problem thoroughly to ensure proper diagnosis and treatment (if applicable).

Table 6.1 Common co-occurring psychological disorders
ASD +

Anxiety disorders:
    social anxiety
    obsessive–compulsive disorder (OCD)
    generalized anxiety disorder
    specific phobia
    panic disorder.

Attention deficit hyperactivity disorder (ADHD)
Tic disorder
Depression
Tourette's disorder

While having awareness of comorbid diagnoses is necessary, it is equally critical to remember that many of these disorders wax and wane—they are not necessarily part of the equation day in and day out and they may improve with treatment. Overall, you should not overly focus on the diagnosis or symptoms such that it becomes a self-fulfilling prophecy— your diagnosis does not define you. With a self-fulfilling

---

5   de Bruin *et al.* (2007)

prophecy, an individual with depression might anticipate that a future episode of depression will occur at the same time of year that they had their last depressive episode—by "expecting" depression to come back, they may look for signs of depression or feel unnecessarily depressed due to overthinking it. Or simply having a diagnosis of ADHD may "enable" someone to feel as if they are not capable of focus or concentration at all and give up prematurely when working on a task requiring concentration.

Seeking Professional Help: Maintaining Emotional Safety

You may work with a mental health team. However, knowing when you need help is difficult to determine, especially if you are in the midst of feeling anxious, unhappy or unsafe. Again, it is better to recruit a mental health professional during times of calm (when things are going well) compared with a crisis, but so often the first time an individual reaches for help is when they are experiencing significant distress. There are several warnings, or "red flags," that may signal to others that you need emotional help (see Tip 6.3). People become especially concerned if multiple red flags are appearing and behaviors and symptoms are unusual or unexpected for you.

TIP 6.3 Mental health red flags

☑ Isolation/loss of interest in others.

☑ Irritability.

☑ Being argumentative with others.

☑ Paranoia.

☑ Significant sleep or dietary changes (or weight loss/gain).

☑ Impaired personal hygiene.

☑ Decline in functioning or performance at work or school.

☑ Drinking/drug use.

☑ Trouble with authority figures (i.e., in trouble with law enforcement, supervisors at work or school).

☑ Changes in personality or behavior.

☑ Self-injurious behavior.

☑ Suicidal talk, gestures or attempts (get help immediately if you are concerned about safety).

Developing a "Team"

Initially when my parents suggested music therapy, I did not want to go. But by giving it a chance, I found something that I now have a passion for. I would also say that finding a good mental health professional is important, but remember, it is personal and you have to connect with the person. You need to click with them and you have to make progress. (Patrick, young adult with ASD)

Finding resources and developing a great team of providers is often key to staying safe and functioning well. However, selecting the professional that is right for you among so many professions and practitioners is a daunting task. When developing a team, a great place to start is to find a qualified resource for mental health (i.e., psychologist, psychiatrist, counselor, social worker, etc.). It is important that you find highly qualified providers and work to find a practitioner who specializes in ASD—and someone who is a good fit. As mentioned earlier, it is much better to have a mental health team in place *before* a crisis as opposed to *during* a crisis (see Tip 6.4). It is also important to find a provider that is a good match. If at first you don't succeed, try, try again (see Tip 6.5).

With respect to *both* physical and emotional health, there are several recommendations that lay the foundation for success. First, if you are experiencing difficulties you should get help—*the professional kind*. It is essential for you (and your support team) to seek professional help when needed. This could pertain to any physical or psychological issue that you may be experiencing. Also, make sure that the help is *good* help. Good, local providers should be found through reputable sources. A non-exhaustive list of clinical providers alongside the credentialing agency is listed in the figure "Guide for potential referrals" and can serve as a method of verifying qualifications (e.g., licensure, board certification, etc.). Remember, asking for help is hard but important.

TIP 6.4 **Developing a good team**

Investigate:

☑ **Your provider**: It is also important to be a good and knowledgeable consumer of mental health services. A good rule of thumb is first to ensure that the provider is licensed or registered (and that their licensure is up to date). You may also want to check to make sure that they are in good standing within their professional association (i.e., for a psychologist, ensuring that they are licensed by the state and that there are no ethical violations associated with their credentials).

☑ **The treatment**: It is also important that the treatment you are receiving is evidence-based and is rooted in a solid foundation of research. It is more challenging to find evidenced based treatments in the teen and adult population with ASD (compared to the child population).[6]

---

6   Mesibov and Shea (2011)

TIP 6.5 Don't give up

Don't get discouraged. Finding a good mental health professional is all about fit. A person may be well qualified and well meaning, but if you feel that they do not understand you or your family, you may not have good success in meeting your treatment goals.

While it is important to give mental health professionals some time (of course, you do not develop a trusting and respected relationship in one session), it is not recommended to stay in a therapy relationship that is not effective.

It can be tempting to assume that all mental health professionals will not be helpful if you have a bad experience—this is a dangerous assumption. Again, do some research, ask friends or professionals for recommendations, even meet with a few potential therapists before committing and try, try again...

Remember:

- **Be proactive**: Don't wait until the last minute to get help. While it is not advised to be overly reactive or catastrophize a minor issue, it is also not recommended that you wait to get help until the problem has become complex and hard to manage.

- **Be open-minded**: Even if you have had a negative experience in the past or are hesitant to try something new, keeping an open mind when you are in need of help is important. Often when individuals need help the most, they are the most resistant to it.

Because there are so many professionals involved with individuals and families with autism, it can be difficult to manage and adhere to all of the recommendations, especially if some contradict one another. It is not unusual to have a primary care physician, a medical specialist physician (e.g., a gastroenterologist or neurologist), a psychiatrist, a psychologist/counselor, a speech and language pathologist and/or a job coach. When paired with some of the planning and organizational challenges that are common, adherence can be a struggle. A trusted family member can often help sort out the various recommendations and help you come to a decision and formulate a treatment plan that works for *you*. Remember the following when developing a treatment plan:

- **Do**: Encourage professionals to communicate about your treatment plan. Making too many changes at once or even getting conflicting recommendations can be very frustrating—it is ethical and good clinical practice to have professionals working together. Note: to facilitate this process, a signed release of information form must be signed.

- **Don't**: Get overwhelmed. While it is important to heed the advice of professionals, it is also important that you all work together in a manner that promotes good communication and meets your treatment goals.

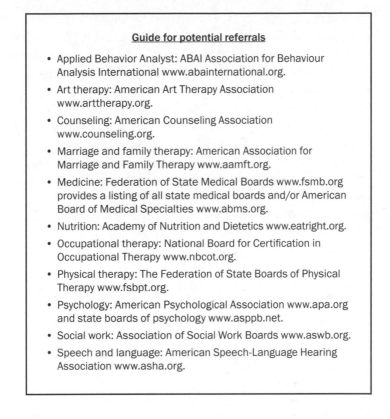

Guide for potential referrals

- Applied Behavior Analyst: ABAI Association for Behaviour Analysis International www.abainternational.org.
- Art therapy: American Art Therapy Association www.arttherapy.org.
- Counseling: American Counseling Association www.counseling.org.
- Marriage and family therapy: American Association for Marriage and Family Therapy www.aamft.org.
- Medicine: Federation of State Medical Boards www.fsmb.org provides a listing of all state medical boards and/or American Board of Medical Specialties www.abms.org.
- Nutrition: Academy of Nutrition and Dietetics www.eatright.org.
- Occupational therapy: National Board for Certification in Occupational Therapy www.nbcot.org.
- Physical therapy: The Federation of State Boards of Physical Therapy www.fsbpt.org.
- Psychology: American Psychological Association www.apa.org and state boards of psychology www.asppb.net.
- Social work: Association of Social Work Boards www.aswb.org.
- Speech and language: American Speech-Language Hearing Association www.asha.org.

Guide for potential referrals

Emotional Resiliency

While prevalence rates of medical and mental health conditions in the ASD population are high, appreciating your resilient nature is important. Resiliency has been identified as one of the key factors to well-being and life satisfaction.[7] Many people encounter challenges in life, but by maintaining

---

7   Luthar (2003)

an optimistic and resilient mentality, you can learn from difficulties and grow from these experiences. Research demonstrates that resiliency is predictive of better outcomes in young adults with ASD, therefore identifying strategies to promote your resilience, like using your emotional intelligence and social support programming, can make a positive impact in your life.[8] Focusing on the positives can help you cope with the negatives. It is often natural to downplay your strengths or engage in self-defeating thinking when you are struggling, but it is essential that you identify and focus on your positive attributes. Thinking about (and writing out) five to ten good characteristics that can be used proactively to manage problems can help you focus on these strengths and plan how to compensate during periods of difficulty (see below).

List of strengths	How strength can help
1	
2	
3	
4	
5	
6	
7	
8	
9	
10	

Identifying strengths for resilience

---

8   Montgomery *et al.* (2008)

Emotion Regulation and Coping Strategies

> Emotions can be totally different for people on the spectrum. If I feel depressed, anxious or angry it feels like "nothing has ever been right." When we are having anxiety attacks, meltdowns, we are telling you exactly how we feel and it's all so consuming. Emotional lines are infinite—I get to thinking that how I am currently feeling is the only way I have ever felt and will feel for eternity. (Aaron, young adult with ASD)

Emotional self-regulation is a skill that many people with ASD find challenging.[9] By understanding emotions and knowing how to respond appropriately, you will be able to prevent and manage negative emotions like stress, anger, anxiety and sadness. The ability to cope with and manage emotions should begin with having awareness of your primary stressors and/or emotional triggers.

Common stressors for young adults with ASD:

- Social situations.
- Relationships.
- School/work responsibilities.
- Deviation from plans/schedule.
- Sensory sensitivities.
- Health concerns (about the individual or a family member).
- Discrimination/bullying.
- Transitions.

---

9   Bachevalier and Loveland (2006)

- Living situations (e.g., roommates, dorm living, living with parents).
- Anticipatory anxiety.

Emotions are certainly difficult to define and interpret, especially for those with ASD.[10] Also, you might experience difficulty in understanding emotions, particularly those of others. When you combine this with sensory sensitivities, the need for sameness and higher rates of emotional distress noted in individuals with ASD, it is understandable that this might result in you being more vulnerable to anger and frustration. Given this heightened vulnerability, it is even *more important* for you to learn ways to self-monitor when it comes to your feelings, particularly anxiety and frustration.

> There used to be a lot of anger in the house for a variety of reasons—personalities, nagging about cleaning up after himself, and general concerns about his laziness at times. However, as a family we have shifted to a "let's agree to disagree" mentality which has helped. I have also moved from nagging to teasing him about his messy room, etc. It helps to make it more of a joke rather than escalating my emotions—which escalates his. (Karen, mother of young adult with ASD)

---

10 Sofronoff *et al.* (2007)

Blowing off Steam

Irritability and frustration are normal emotions in young adulthood—based, in part, on the natural desire for independence, the challenges of figuring out one's own identity and the enhanced cognitive capabilities that result in critical thinking. These normative developmental processes naturally lead to increased thought-provoking discussions and more heated arguments. An additional part of the frustration equation is linked to temperamental and personality characteristics. As articulated in the quote from Karen, the awareness that her son and husband tend to be argumentative and irritable by nature is an important dynamic to recognize. Understanding the problem allowed Karen to develop a way to adapt to the situation. By changing *her* mindset and understanding this dynamic, Karen was able to set realistic expectations, which helped her cope with the situation. Additionally, she went on to note that changing her behaviors (e.g., not escalating the situation and finding ways to turn her frustration into humor) reduced her frustration. Most importantly, you need to recognize the symptoms and feelings you experience when you are angry and do your very best to manage these in a productive manner, before you blow off steam in a non-healthy way. Take a look at the figures "Blowing off steam" and "Articulating and recognizing escalating feelings," which act as a guide to assist you in identifying your feelings and "catching" yourself before the lid pops off!

Blowing off steam

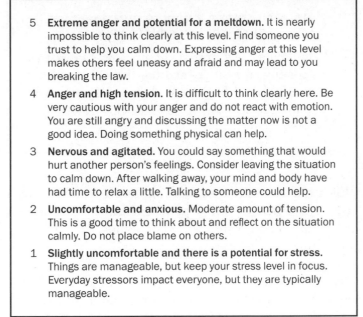

5   **Extreme anger and potential for a meltdown.** It is nearly impossible to think clearly at this level. Find someone you trust to help you calm down. Expressing anger at this level makes others feel uneasy and afraid and may lead to you breaking the law.

4   **Anger and high tension.** It is difficult to think clearly here. Be very cautious with your anger and do not react with emotion. You are still angry and discussing the matter now is not a good idea. Doing something physical can help.

3   **Nervous and agitated.** You could say something that would hurt another person's feelings. Consider leaving the situation to calm down. After walking away, your mind and body have had time to relax a little. Talking to someone could help.

2   **Uncomfortable and anxious.** Moderate amount of tension. This is a good time to think about and reflect on the situation calmly. Do not place blame on others.

1   **Slightly uncomfortable and there is a potential for stress.** Things are manageable, but keep your stress level in focus. Everyday stressors impact everyone, but they are typically manageable.

Articulating and recognizing escalating feelings

Articulating One's Feelings

Once you are able to self-monitor your feelings and emotions, communicating about these emotions to others in an appropriate manner is the next step (see Social Script 6.2). Labeling an emotion allows you delicately (and accurately) communicate your feelings and triggers,[11] and can be the first step in helping others better understand your individual needs.

---

11 Triggers are actions, words, places or events that are known to cause you distress.

**SOCIAL SCRIPT 6.2 HOW TO COMMUNICATE
THAT YOU ARE FRUSTRATED**

"I am feeling really frustrated right now. I know that it is coming off as angry and hostile but when I feel this way I find it helpful to take a break and spend some time alone. Can we continue this conversation at another time?"

When you accurately articulate your feelings and emotional needs to others, it helps prevent misunderstandings or misinterpretations. Expressing your feelings to others and advocating your needs are essential ways to prevent anger outbursts that might alarm other people. Being able to communicate that you are frustrated and need time alone is preferred to exploding or having a meltdown. If and when you are frustrated, that frustration may be expressed in an unhealthy way that is scary to those observing (e.g., pacing, self-stimulatory behaviors, yelling/screaming). Attempting to communicate at the first sign of frustration, as opposed to during the height of anger and frustration, will allow you to avoid potential safety issues (e.g., scaring others, causing a scene, having to interact with police) that occur as a result of poor emotion regulation. When another person, versus an event, is the source of the angry feeling or is engaging in a behavior that is frustrating, it is better to address the behavior calmly and directly (see Social Script 6.3).

If someone is frustrating you, just pull them to the side and state the situation. Don't beat around the bush. State it outright and say why it affected you so much. Once you make that anger known, you can find ways to fix the problem. Let others know how you're feeling. Just acknowledge what happened and move on. I think it is important to not beat around the bush; state the situation clearly and tell them why it bothered you so it does not happen again. Just as important is *moving on* once you have addressed it. It does no good to dwell on it. (Dave, young adult with ASD)

SOCIAL SCRIPT 6.3 COMMUNICATING YOUR NEEDS WHEN FRUSTRATED OR ANGRY

Note: it may be wise to have this conversation away from other people.

Stephen: "Hey man, can I talk to you for a second?"

Mickey: "Sure, I guess."

Stephen: "I just wanted to let you know that I didn't like the way you (fill in the blank). Next time, I would appreciate it if (fill in the blank)."

Coping Skills and Stress Management

I immerse myself in the things that I enjoy and it's relaxing for me. I love music and am good at music so I just choose to focus on the things I enjoy, that I am good at. I need to make sure that I can go to that space and reset myself. (Aaron, young adult with ASD)

Finding strategies to promote effective coping and emotion regulation is necessary for your quality of life and the quality of your relationships with others. Emotional/physical well-being and safety are also enhanced when you practice good emotional regulation. Good coping skills not only prevent problems from occurring, but they can also assist in managing and reducing emotionally based issues. For some, coping skills can be physical in nature, for example, relaxation breathing, yoga or exercise. For others, relaxation is more of a cognitive process that includes meditation, guided imagery, journaling or positive self-talk. It is also helpful to make time on a daily basis for activities that are stress reducing in nature and that bring you joy.

> For me, video games are my source of relaxation. It just makes everything disappear for me. A lot of other people seem to find working out relaxing. I think too much when I work out. I would rather play video games or throw a rubber ball against the wall 50–100 times. (Alex, young adult with ASD)

Remember, what works for one person, may not work for you. Similarly, depending on the situation or the severity, you may need different strategies (or a combination of strategies) to cope effectively. The figure "Healthy coping skills and stress relievers" provides a short list of coping skills that may be beneficial.

HEALTHY COPING SKILLS AND STRESS RELIEVERS

- Listening to music.
- Exercise.
- Deep breathing.
- Journaling.
- Reading a book or magazine.
- Playing a video game.
- Yoga.
- Getting in touch with nature.
- Artwork.
- Taking a nap.
- Swinging or jumping on a trampoline.

Self-esteem and Self-concept

We must give individuals with autism the respect and dignity that they deserve. They are capable and valued. Individuals with autism are among the most wonderful and interesting people who help me view the world from a unique and fun-loving perspective. Individuals with ASD need to get educated in school and get a career and if they don't have the skills to get to the next stage, they will get depressed. It is essential to get up with a purpose in the morning—this could be school, a job, a volunteer position. I worked with a young man, Jimmy, who worked in a factory and made boxes. Regularly, his supervisor would document his accomplishments in a way that made Jimmy feel such pride—"Jimmy made 500 boxes today—that is a lot of boxes!" He would share his daily achievement with me, demonstrating his pride. (Maryann, respite service provider)

For many, preventing depression and promoting mental health are related to a sense of self and pride in what you do and who you are (see the figure "Sources of self-esteem"). Thus, if you are underemployed, socially frustrated and isolated and not being challenged in your daily activities, it is easy to feel depressed and frustrated. While this topic is too broad and far reaching for this book, it deserves mention. In the absence of understanding the larger issues, individuals and families may be unsuccessfully implementing strategies to improve physical and mental health and failing. Finding ways to improve self-esteem, enhance feelings of pride and facilitate short- and long-term goals is an essential part of self-actualization (i.e., achieving your idealizing self and living up to your potential). Prolonged periods of time that are unproductive and under-stimulating contribute to feelings of depression, isolation and loneliness.

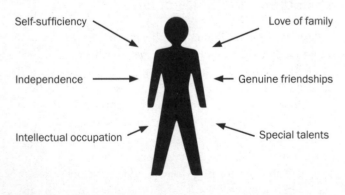

Sources of self-esteem

Social Support

For me, what helped me manage my emotions was hitting bottom. Everyone has his/her own bottom. For me, I was at a place where I didn't like where I was and was on the verge of depression. I just started to let go of my baggage. Everyone has to have a go-to person to vent and let it all out. I realized that I can't do it all on my own and need others there for me. I am very big on affection; I love to give and receive affections, give hugs. It's incredible how a simple hug or kind words can be extremely uplifting. For me, it's never keeping things to yourself. It's all about expressing your feelings, like anger, and getting it all out. You need to approach the things that cause you stress and mediate the problem. (Dave, young adult with ASD)

Mental Health and Well-being

I am 24 years old, so it is natural that I don't want to listen to what my parents are telling me to do. I want to be independent and make my own decisions but that can cause conflict sometimes. (Alex, young adult with ASD)

The mental and physical health of the family is essential and must be examined. As reflected in the above quote from Alex, it can be stressful for young adults to live with family (regardless of any ASD diagnosis), *and* it can be frustrating for the family as well. Finding ways to negotiate living with one another and supporting each other is essential.

In the midst of the daily grind and implementing all of the advice you have been given from friends, family and professionals, it is easy to minimize your needs for health and happiness. It is also easy to forget to have fun.

Families should ensure that they work hard on fostering important relationships and communication among family members, while also taking time to practice good self-care. A number of families find valuable resources in the community that share ideas, support, education and a short but valuable respite—help your family realize that while helping you, they must also take time to practice good self-care! As is often said, a chain is only as strong as its weakest link. The health and well-being of your family or support team is an important component of the larger picture for you.

Maintaining Good Physical Health

While coping skills are great, preventing problems by eating right, exercising regularly and getting enough sleep is preferable. You want to maintain a healthy routine, including eating nutritious meals, engaging in regular exercise, getting sufficient sleep and maintaining personal hygiene. In addition to staying healthy in order to optimize performance, stay alert and feel good, you can also benefit from the routine and structure associated with self-care and living independently. Adjusting to independence as a young adult will require that you monitor your health in proactive and conscientious ways. In the following sections we review the areas of concern around maintaining good health.

Healthy and balanced eating

Once my young adult clients are on their own, they have terrible diets—eating whatever they want. They get into a routine and then it is set and it can be dangerous (Snickers bar at break every day). I see more kids being negatively impacted by diet. Anyone that ate that way would have poor side effects. It's really figuring out how to increase acceptance of different foods. Showing recipes that are attached to their favorite shows or movies seems to help such as the Harry Potter cookbook. They are more likely to eat that if it comes out of the book. You have to be creative in getting them to eat a more balanced diet. (Beth Thompson, Milestones Autism Resources Teen/Adult Services Manager, social worker with specialization in young adults with autism)

Eating "right," that is, a diet inclusive of a range of foods and within a specific calorie range based on height, weight and activity level, is a precursor to maintaining your physical and psychological well-being. While the link between diet and physical health is more obvious, eating habits also impact mood, the ability to sustain attention, energy levels and cognitive processing skills.

However, the sensory sensitivities associated with ASD, and the preference for repetition and sameness, can have a negative impact on your diet. You may have a very limited number of foods or types of foods that you enjoy. Or you may struggle with food choices and need assistance to incorporate healthy eating strategies into your daily lifestyle, while being mindful of dietary preferences and restrictions. You may even have specific dietary restrictions based on allergies or personal preference. While gluten- and casein-free diets are widespread, there is limited empirical evidence to support their use to reduce ASD symptoms.[12] New diets, or the decision to restrict the intake of an entire food "type," should only happen under the care of a physician. Regardless of the type of diet or the rationale for selecting it, the overarching safety concern is your nutritional status.

---

12 Milward *et al.* (2008)

Selective eating is one of the most common eating problems for individuals with ASD and can negatively impact health and well-being.[13] On the other hand, overeating is also a common problem in this population and can cause other health problems including weight gain and obesity, heart disease, tooth decay and diabetes. For many, the eating challenges are directly related to sensory sensitivities surrounding eating (e.g., olfactory (smell, touch, taste), tactile and gustatory sensitivities), preference for routine, medications, gastrointestinal problems, motor challenges and restrictive patterns of interests. Some suggest that "individuals with ASD may have their own ideas on nutrition…and do not feel, or do not attend to feelings of hunger and satiety, or to the pleasure of eating."[14]

SOME CONSIDERATIONS AROUND RESTRICTIVE EATING

- Atypical and restrictive eating can have a negative impact on physical health.

- Atypical and restrictive eating can have a negative impact on energy, concentration and mood.

- Some young adults with ASD may have difficulty interpreting internal cues for hunger, satiety (i.e., fullness) or thirst. Abnormal sensations of hunger and satiety as well as disordered eating seem to be common in ASD and entail the risk of both over- and under-eating. (Rastam 2008)

Due to the frequency and severity of eating challenges in ASD and the serious impact eating challenges can have on your

---

13 Rastam (2008)
14 Rastam (2008) p.35

health, developing strategies to maintain or improve your eating habits is essential.

CHANGES IN DIET

Small changes in diet and healthy approaches to food can help you feel better. Planning meals in advance, writing down a shopping list, going to the grocery store and cooking at home can greatly decrease your monthly food expenses and are more likely to result in healthier choices compared with eating fast food or going out to a restaurant. Instead of relying on takeout, you can prepare home-cooked meals for yourself and enjoy a healthier lifestyle. Even though you might enjoy eating fast food and candy, or other "junk food," a regular diet of these foods can be risky. Like Patrick, you can manage your diet by making healthier choices (see Tip 6.7).

> I don't have any specific food sensitivities, but I do try to make better food choices like grilled chicken instead of breaded, and I avoid empty calories from alcohol and soda. (Patrick, young adult with ASD)

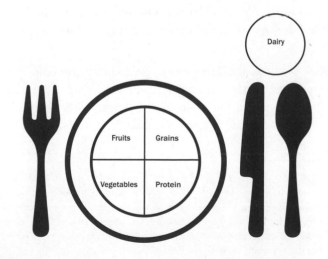

MyPlate

TIP 6.7 **Recommendations for eating challenges**

☑ Familiarize yourself with the food plate[15] (see the figure "MyPlate") and healthy eating habits for your body.

☑ Consult with medical professionals about diet-related concerns.

☑ Compensate for restricted diet through the use of vitamins and supplements (e.g., Boost, Ensure, etc.) under the supervision of a medical professional.

☑ Plan meals in advance, keeping MyPlate and/or professional recommendations in mind.

☑ When possible, avoid fast food and eating out.

☑ If you are a restrictive eater, attempt to slowly introduce new foods into the weekly meal plan.

☑ If support and assistance is needed to expand food choices, consult with professionals.

☑ Consult a dietician/nutritionist for more individualized assistance with general meal planning and nutrition goals.

☑ www.choosemyplate.gov is a great interactive (and free) website to assist with daily food plans, sample menus and tips for eating healthy on a budget. Other helpful websites include: www.hc-sc.gc.ca/fn-an/food-guide-

---

15 MyPlate (formerly the food pyramid) was developed in 1992 by the United States Food and Drug Administration as a model for healthy eating. The pyramid had six vertical sections representing the five food groups plus fats/oils (fruits, vegetables, protein, dairy, and bread) and made recommendations regarding the recommended servings of each per day) (Welsh, Davis and Shaw, 1992).

aliment/basics-base/quantit-eng.php, www.eatwell.gov. uk and www.eatforhealth.gov.au.

My son participated in a weight management program through our regional university hospital and had success in losing nearly 30 pounds. As a family we were educated about "sometimes" foods versus "daily" foods, which helped him make better choices with respect to foods. We were not making progress by doing it alone and decided to get professional help. (Mother of young adult with ASD)

The United States Department of Agriculture (USDA) has recently modified the food pyramid and replaced it with "My Plate," which outlines the recommended types and ratios of food types per day. "My Plate" is a convenient and visual representation of guidelines for healthy eating. In simplistic terms, it is recommended that half of the "plate" be filled with fruits and vegetables while the other half of the plate should be split between grains and proteins. In the "My Plate" visual, there is a cup representing the importance of having limited quantities of dairy (i.e., milk, cheese, yogurt) in the diet as well. The take-home message from these recent USDA guidelines is to have lots of fruits and vegetables with smaller amounts of grains, protein and dairy to have a well-balanced diet that promotes a healthy weight.

When taken to the extreme, eating challenges can quickly develop into more serious eating disorders (e.g., anorexia nervosa, bulimia nervosa, etc.), particularly if not addressed. Eating problems, such as feeding difficulties, pica, eating disorders and overeating, are important issues related to ASD and should be closely monitored by a medical professional due to the inherent safety concerns associated with poor nutrition.

Sleep and Sleep Hygiene

> I do not sleep (well). I'm sort of nocturnal, so finding a time that works for me to fall asleep helps the rest of the cycle fall into place. Part of my difficulty is trying to fit my schedule into a schedule that works. Since I'm more productive at night, a third shift job is best for me. While I might not sleep for eight hours a day, the ability to sleep "when I can" and when I am most likely to sleep (during the day) helps me function. (Aaron, young adult with ASD)

Getting a good night's rest can make the difference between a good day and a horrible day. The recommended daily amount of sleep for essential functioning is seven to nine hours (per day) for young adults.[16] Maintaining a regular sleep schedule that accommodates a reasonable and healthy duration of sleep is essential to building your resiliency, minimizing the effects of stressors and enhancing proper brain functioning. Unfortunately, you may not be getting enough sleep, especially in an independent setting like college or apartment building where noise levels cannot always be controlled. Staying up late every once in a while is not a bad thing, but should also not be the norm. Lack of sleep can lead to potentially negative consequences. For example, someone who stayed awake all night playing video games might accidentally sleep through an important appointment or class the following day. Driving, working and even tasks like cooking can be more difficult when you experience a lack of sleep and can compromise your safety in a variety of ways.

---

16 National Sleep Federation (2015)

Almost 80 percent of individuals with ASD experience sleep disturbances.[17] The most common sleep challenges and disorders include: insomnia, difficulty falling asleep, night waking, sleepwalking, night terrors and sleep apnea. Even without a diagnosable sleep disorder, you may be like others on the spectrum who have notoriously poor sleep hygiene— they stay up too late, eat in bed, watch television to fall asleep and have irregular wake times and sleep times. These sleep issues are often exacerbated if you have sensory sensitivities, medical and emotional comorbidities and/or restrictive/ repetitive behaviors. When it comes to safety, you should recognize the impact sleep has on the body and how serious the implications of a sleep-deprived state can be. Consequences of sleep deprivation range from sleepiness and irritability to more significant challenges such as memory loss, vulnerability to accidents and increased risk for chronic health conditions like stroke, hypertension, obesity and diabetes.[18] Also, medication side effects, medical problems and emotional issues (e.g., depression or anxiety) can contribute to sleeping difficulties and should be communicated to the healthcare team.

Note: It is critical to consult with a medical professional regarding sleep and related disorders. Again, there may be medical conditions that can explain sleep disorders, and sleep disorders can cause or exacerbate medical conditions.

BEHAVIORAL CONTROLS

Understanding and practicing good sleep hygiene can help prevent sleep problems or can provide a relatively simple solution to existing problems. Sleep hygiene refers to establishing routines and practices in your environment

17 Richdale (1999)
18 Alvarez and Ayas (2004)

that help promote sleep, ranging from limiting caffeine to creating a sleeping environment with minimal distractions. According to the National Sleep Foundation, some standard recommendations for sleep hygiene include the following:

- Avoid sleeping during the day (i.e., naps).

- Limit caffeine intake.

- Establish a bedtime routine that is consistent and relaxing.

- Use your bed only for sleep—avoid watching television, eating or working on the computer and maintain a sleeping environment that is calming and relaxing.

- Exposure to natural light can help promote a healthy sleep–wake cycle, as can regular exercise.

- Try to maintain consistent sleep and wake times when possible.

(Hirshkowitz et al. 2015)

Establishing a bedtime routine is also great way to promote good sleep. For some it may be taking a shower before bed, dimming the lights an hour before bed, getting into pajamas or playing relaxing music. A familiar bedtime routine helps cue your body, in tandem with biological cues, to feel sleepy and promote rest. Also, while napping during the day is tempting, it can make it very difficult to sleep at night—especially when you have sleep challenges. This can lead to a negative pattern of sleepless nights and unproductive days. It is difficult but necessary to break this cycle. Getting into good sleep habits can be an easy way to improve your physical and emotional health.

PHYSICAL ENVIRONMENT

Ensuring that the physical environment of the sleeping space is sensory neutral will help to promote healthy sleeping patterns. Some environmental considerations include:

- temperature of the room
- lighting
- clothing
- white noise (i.e., fan, sound machine)
- bedding (texture, patterns, etc.)
- décor and amount of clutter
- mattress (soft or firm).

If you are not getting enough sleep you should isolate the cause and attempt to find a solution. Sometimes finding the right temperature, having the perfectly fluffy pillow, listening to music or stretching on a yoga mat before bed can be easy solutions to an uneasy rest.

Barrier to getting good sleep	Possible solutions
Sensitivity to light	Room-darkening shades; use of eye mask
Distracted by noises	Use of white noise or relaxing music; having thick carpeting and other sound-absorbing material in the room
Hard time falling asleep due to racing thoughts	Use of mindfulness meditation; reading a relaxing book before bed
Hard time falling asleep (general)	Using bed exclusively for sleep
Not tired	Ensure you are getting enough exercise during the day; stay away from caffeine; avoid sleeping during the day

Barrier to getting good sleep	Possible solutions
Irregular sleep patterns due to a job or living arrangement	Try to maintain a regular sleep and wake schedule if possible; use room-darkening shades if you need to sleep during the day
Texture-based discomfort	Address bedding and sleepwear; consult with professionals about sensory sensitivities

Sometimes the cause of sleep challenges is not obvious and professional consultation is needed. Similarly, the treatment of sleep issues for young adults with autism is often complex because of co-occurring challenges that cannot be addressed solely by changing the bedtime routine or altering the sleep environment. If you continue to have sleep issues seek professional health from your physician.

Physical Activity and Exercise

> We decided to invest in getting him a personal trainer, which really helped him to learn how to use the equipment independently (he has hypotonia) and to overcome other strength issues which were barriers for exercise. (Mother of young adult with ASD)

In addition to eating well, it is important for you to get regular exercise. Exercise can help maintain a healthy, conditioned and strong body. The best way to begin exercising is to ease into it by taking some time each day to go on a short walk, taking the stairs rather than elevators/escalators and/or incorporating some additional movement into day-to-day tasks. For tracking purposes, it can be helpful to begin recording the number of steps taken daily with a pedometer or related device. In fact, many smartphones have applications that can monitor movement and other fitness parameters.

In addition to being active throughout daily activities, you can work to develop regular exercise routines. While some people are more comfortable exercising indoors at a gym or within the comforts of their own home, others have a preference for outdoor activities, like hiking or biking. No matter what your personal preference is, there are options.

CONSIDERATIONS ABOUT PHYSICAL EXERCISE

- **Overall health:** There are benefits to any form of exercise, but it's important to consult with a doctor about the best option when considering your age, health status and fitness goals.

- **Fitness level:** Try to find a challenging, yet manageable form of exercise; if beginning a new fitness regime, start slowly and seek consultation if experiencing any health concerns.

- **Type of workout:** From walking to yoga to kickboxing, there are seemingly endless ways to get in some regular exercise.

- **Knowledge/familiarity:** If you are interested in joining an exercise club, but are intimidated by the equipment, etc., it may be a good idea to work for a few sessions with a personal trainer to get familiar or join an exercise class with a trained instructor.

- **Financial considerations:** If you cannot afford a gym membership, there will be a wide array of fitness videos available for rent at your local library.

- **Privacy versus being social:** Being a member at a gym might afford you more opportunities to meet people, while exercising at home is private. Select the option that is most appealing.

- **Remember that gyms often play loud music to "pump people up:"** In addition, lighting in gyms tends to be bright and florescent and gyms smell of sweat and body odor. If these types of sensory issues bother you, you may want to consider avoiding the gym and opting for a home fitness machine or a smaller, more private gym.

- **If the sensory issues or social aspects of a gym are overwhelming,** you can try an exercise DVD or develop an independent workout plan.

Having fitness goals can be useful for motivation and focus. For example, working with a professional related to your goal weight based on your body mass index (BMI), a fitness goal (e.g., running a 10k race) or fitting into a certain size of clothing. Some individuals have success in launching their own fitness/diet regimen while others benefit from the structure of a weight-loss program (e.g., Weight Watchers, Jenny Craig, etc.) or by enlisting the help of fitness or medical professionals. Choose the plan that is right for you by knowing your preferences, researching programs and talking to your doctor.

Note: Body mass index (BMI) is an index of body fat based on weight and height. A healthy BMI ranges from 18.5 to 24.9 There are many free online BMI calculators that can be used by the general public, but in general BMI is calculated by using the following equation: weight(kg)/height(m)^2.

BMI CATEGORIES

- Underweight: less than 18.5.
- **Healthy: 18.5 to 24.9.**
- Overweight: 25 to 29.9.
- Obese: over 30.

Summary

Maintaining good health and managing stress are very important for happiness, quality of life and safety. There are many components to both the prevention and management of health-related problems, but developing skills and strategies is a smart investment of your time and energy. Further, being able to address medical needs independently, like self-advocating with the medical team, taking medications as directed, storing medications properly and understanding your treatments, is essential. Also, developing advanced skills in emotional regulation and stress-management strategies can lead to life-long advantages and well-being. Even more helpful, the prevention of stress and anxiety by ensuring proper diet, sleep and physical activity can help you maintain emotional and physical health and stay safe.

References

Alvarez, G. G. and Ayas, N. T. (2004) 'The impact of daily sleep duration on health: A review of the literature.' *Progress in Cardiovascular Nursing 19,* 2, 56–59.

Bachevalier, J. and Loveland, K. A. (2006) 'The orbitofrontal–amygdala circuit and self-regulation of social-emotional behavior in autism.' *Neuroscience and Biobehavioral Reviews 30,*1, 97–117.

de Bruin, E. I., Ferdinand, R. F., Meester, S., de Nijs, P. F. and Verheij, F. (2007) 'High rates of psychiatric co-morbidity in PDD-NOS.' *Journal of Autism and Developmental Disorders 37,* 5, 877–886.

Hirshkowitz, M., Whiton, K., Albert, S. M., Alessi, C. et al. (2015) 'National Sleep Foundation's sleep time duration recommendations: Methodology and results summary.' *Sleep Health 1,* 1, 40–43.

Kohane, I. S., McMurry, A., Weber, G., MacFadden, D. et al. (2012) 'The co-morbidity burden of children and young adults with autism spectrum disorders.' *PloS one 7,* 4, e33224–e33224.

Luthar, S. S. (2003) *Resilience and Vulnerability: Adaptation in the Context of Childhood Adversities.* New York: Cambridge University Press.

Mesibov, G. B. and Shea, V. (2011) 'Evidence-based practices and autism.' *Autism 15,* 1, 114–133.

Millward, C., Ferriter, M., Calver, S. and Connell-Jones, G. (2008) 'Gluten- and casein-free diets for autistic spectrum disorder.' Cochrane Database of Systematic Reviews, 2, 2.

Montgomery, J. M., Schwean, V. L., Burt, J. A. G., Dyke, D. I. *et al.* (2008) 'Emotional intelligence and resiliency in young adults with Asperger's disorder: Challenges and opportunities.' *Canadian Journal of School Psychology 23*, 1, 70–93.

National Sleep Federation (2015) *How Much Sleep Do You Need?* Arlington, VA: National Sleep Federation. Available at http://sleepfoundation.org/how-sleep-works/how-much-sleep-do-we-really-need, accessed on 1 November 2015.

Petrovic, S. and Petrovic, D. (2014) *Expect a Miracle: A Mother/Son Asperger Journey of Determination and Triumph.* West Conshohocken, PA: Infinity Publishing.

Rastam, M. (2008) 'Eating disturbances in autism spectrum disorders with focus on adolescent and adult years.' *Clinical Neuropsychiatry 5*, 1, 31–42.

Richdale, A. L. (1999) 'Sleep problems in autism: Prevalence, cause, and intervention.' *Developmental Medicine and Child Neurology 41*,1, 60–66.

Rigler, M., Rutherford, A. and Quinn, E. (2015) *Developing Identity, Strengths, and Self-perception for Young Adults with Autism Spectrum Disorder: The BASICS College Curriculum.* London: Jessica Kingsley Publishers.

Sofronoff, K., Attwood, T., Hinton, S. and Levin, I. (2007) 'A randomized controlled trial of a cognitive behavioral intervention for anger management in children diagnosed with Asperger syndrome.' *Journal of Autism and Developmental Disorders 37*, 7, 1203–1214.

Welsh, S., Davis, C. and Shaw, A. (1992) 'Development of the food guide pyramid.' *Nutrition Today 27*, 6, 12–23.

PART THREE

Independent Living

Chapter 7

Don't Touch my Things

Independent Living and Roommates

★ Independent living skills.

★ Roommate selection/agreement.

★ Triggers.

★ Trust.

I am 24 years old, so it is natural that I don't want to listen to what my parents are telling me to do. I want to be independent and make my own decisions. I would like to move out but I am not ready; hopefully in two years. I know that I need social support (i.e., true friends and family) and a location I like; it also needs to be affordable. I am doing the things I need to do now to get ready for moving out. I am pushing myself to get out there and learn to make friends. I learned from the experience living on campus in college that I do better when I have people that I can socialize with that KNOW ME. (Alex, young adult with ASD)

Transitioning to Living Independently

Residential independence has long been a key indicator for the successful transition into adulthood,[1] however the timeline for entry into independent living is often extended when you have autism. A tough job market and barriers to employment such as difficulty with interviews, socialization, transportation or sensory issues force many young adults to remain home or return home after living independently for a period of time. While you may be less likely to live independently—it is more important to develop strategies specific to your lifestyle that will promote independence and safety.

Living at Home

> Neal lives with me and his brother; primarily because of financial reasons (saving money by living at home) and also because of the challenges I have seen in higher education with individuals with ASD. It is hard to change school and the living situation all at once—change is hard at baseline for kids with ASD. (Anne, mother of young adult with ASD)

Almost 42 percent of neuro-typical adults between the ages of 20 and 24 years old live with their parents.[2] While this living arrangement is a great way for you and your family to save money while managing the transition process in a safe way, this method could also potentially create frustration. For example, this living situation might create an internal conflict for you if you crave independence but are not quite comfortable or ready to live on your own. Educating yourself

---

1   Anderson *et al.* (2014)
2   Aud, KewalRamani and Frohlich (2011)

about the adaptive life skills necessary to move into the next phase of independent living is essential. Whether living at home is your short- or long-term plan, developing strategies that promote safe and independent living is a wise investment. While you may not want or choose to live independently, this chapter highlights some safety concerns for those who do and for those who are navigating cohabitation with family or a roommate.

> I have lived with my mom in my same house for my whole life. That is my routine and where I feel safe. I will move away from there someday but I don't think I'm ready right now, but I'm working on it. (MM, young adult with ASD)

Skills for Independent Living

Several of the necessary skills for independent living are listed below. Practicing these skills while living at home is a great way for you to ensure a more successful transition to residential independence. While at home you should assess your skill level based on the list of *Emerging Skills Needed for Independent Living* below. Develop a plan to develop these skills for yourself with less guidance than you are used to. This list is a stepping-stone; however, as the level of your independence increases, so should the expectations for that independence.

EMERGING SKILLS NEEDED FOR INDEPENDENT LIVING

- Communication/conflict management.
- Money management.
- Transportation skills.
- Medication management.

- Healthy eating.
- Wellness.
- Time management.
- Cooking.
- Cleaning.

Housing Options

When it comes to housing, there are multiple options that you may want to try out. While many young adults are living with parents, siblings or other relatives, some reside in group homes or supported housing. Perhaps you plan to pursue, or are already pursuing, postsecondary education and living in residence halls, either with or without roommates. You might also choose to live independently either alone or with a roommate. No matter what the living situation, there are both quality of life and safety concerns that are important for you to consider.

Roommates

Living with a roommate can be a natural first step towards adulthood, autonomy and independence. You may live with roommates for a number of reasons, and many of these arrangements can have positive impacts on your socialization skills and your adjustment to living independently.[3] It is normal to feel a bit stressed and overwhelmed during the transition to living independently, especially if you will be living with someone new. Due to the transition-related

---

3   Rigler, Rutherford and Quinn (2015)

challenges for individuals on the spectrum, you may find the initial adjustment to be more difficult than it is for others. Therefore, implementing strategies and preparing in advance for what having a roommate could be like are essential.

Having roommates requires some planning and discussion around sharing a common space and the associated responsibilities (e.g., cleaning, cooking, financial contributions, etc.). Knowing what to expect, managing conflict when it occurs and establishing and respecting personal privacy and boundaries are necessary in order to have a successful partnership with your roommate. Work with your roommate to develop guidelines for your living arrangement including rules for shared spaces, cleaning, etc. It is also important for your safety and that of your roommate to review safety plans and procedures. There are numerous issues to consider, for example, if it is important for you to have your own space that your roommate does not have access to, stating that in the beginning will help alleviate the potential for an argument later. If you have food allergies, it is important to discuss these with your roommate to avoid any potential allergic reactions or sickness. If you are averse to having a weapon in your home, sharing this with a potential roommate will be vital.

> I have lived with roommates my entire time in college and most of the experiences have been good, except for this last semester. I had a roommate that was younger than us and drank a lot of alcohol. We are not even supposed to have alcohol in our dorms so this made me really anxious. All my roommates argued all the time and even though I had my own bedroom, I could never really escape all the noise. I finally went to my Residence Director for help with managing all this. (EM, young adult with ASD)

Choosing a Roommate

Choosing a roommate can be a daunting task but it is important to be thorough during the process. You must have realistic expectations about what it will be like to live with a new person, and you must understand your triggers and understand how to avoid or cope with these. It may be important to communicate your triggers or other unique issues to your roommates so they will be equipped to cope with them as well. Finally, you have to be able to understand boundaries, trust and the many responsibilities of being a roommate.

Once you have decided on a potential roommate, that person should be consulted to gauge their interest in a shared living situation. This conversation could be difficult if the other person is not interested in sharing living space. It could feel uncomfortable if someone rejects your inquiry, however, their decision should never be taken personally (see Social Script 7.1). Practicing this conversation prior to asking the other person could alleviate some of the pressure.

SOCIAL SCRIPT 7.1 ASKING SOMEONE TO BE YOUR ROOMMATE

"(Name), we have known each other for a long time and I know a lot about you. We play many of the same games and know a lot of the same people. But, also, you know a lot about the sensory issues I have with my living space. I am ready to move out and am looking for a roommate. I think we would be a good match because we already know one another and have an established trust. Would you consider being my roommate?"

Realistic Expectations

Living with other people can be fun, exhausting and confusing all at the same time. In addition to adjusting to the responsibilities associated with independent living, you may be challenged by some of the social elements involved in living with roommates. Most people, regardless of whether or not they are on the spectrum, struggle with having a roommate. There are many concerns that need to be addressed prior to moving into a shared living space with another person.

CONCERNS AROUND REALISTIC EXPECTATIONS

- Roommates don't have the same expectations for cleanliness.

- Roommates don't have the same expectations for noise levels in the home.

- Roommates don't have similar social expectations.

- Roommates don't have similar privacy expectations.

- Roommates don't share in similar sleep patterns.

- Roommates don't agree on the allowance of pets.

- Roommates don't share the same expectation for environmental factors (water usage, electricity, recycling, etc.).

Developing an understanding of these common issues and including them in a roommate agreement can help alleviate the stress that comes along with a new living situation. It can be complicated, but it can also be a rewarding experience. Having realistic expectations for your living arrangements can help you navigate the situation with confidence.

Know your Triggers

Everyone lives in their own little world and the hard part of communication with a roommate or someone you are living with is translating the way you see the world into a way that they can understand it and vice versa. It's the same with international symbols and gestures. How we view what other people say or do towards us is important. The lens that I receive information through is shaded and I have to compensate for that. (Aaron, young adult with ASD)

Having a solid relationship with a roommate prior to moving in together is often more successful than moving in with a stranger, for a variety of reasons. An established relationship with another person can help you mitigate some of the issues inherent in getting to know someone's habits such as if they are clean or messy, a night owl or an early bird. In addition, having an established relationship with another person increases the likelihood that they understand your unique personality, needs and preferences. Whether your needs have to do with your preference for consistent habits and routines or are more focused on sensory issues in the living environment, having a roommate who already understands the impact ASD may have on your daily life can make this transition a much more positive experience. It is a good idea to have a conversation with your potential roommate(s) (prior to moving in together) about why he or she would be a good roommate for you and why you would be a good roommate for him/her.

As mentioned above, openly discussing triggers, or the things that really upset or frustrate you, and how you choose to deal with these can be very helpful when it comes to managing conflict. While Neal, a young adult with ASD, lives with his mom and brother to save money, conflicts have occurred because of communication differences, but once these were discussed, they found a communication style that works well for them.

> I prefer that my mom texts me questions she has, even when we're home together. It gives me a chance to control my response and avoid being frustrated by interruptions. I don't like it when she calls to me from downstairs, so I told her about it and we worked out a system of communication that works for us to better manage conflict. (Neal, young adult with ASD)

Living with other people, whether it is a roommate or a family member, can be difficult, but escalated, frustrating situations can be avoided if everyone shares their communication preferences and expectations around handling conflict. For example, if you know that you are sensitive to loud music, you can communicate this to your roommates in advance so that they avoid playing their music too loud in the common area. When people are aware of your triggers, or strong preferences and potential issues, they can adjust their behavior accordingly. In the absence of this understanding, a conflict could occur because the roommate was unaware of your potential triggers. It is important to keep in mind that even if you share information about triggers and make your preferences known, it does not mean that problems won't occur. Ultimately, it is always your responsibility to manage your reaction to triggers.

Trust

Trust is among the most important aspects of living with other people. You should be able to feel comfortable in your own home. Home is often considered a "safe space" and should be a place where you can feel relaxed. When choosing to live with a roommate, you will need to build trust with that roommate so that everyone feels safe in the home. Trust can be accomplished through the established and agreed upon guidelines, but building trust takes time and experience and goes far beyond any roommate agreement. In the beginning of a new living situation, you should practice "guarded" trust with your roommate. This means you should not automatically distrust or trust the other person, but approach certain things with caution. For example, prescription medications should be locked up, as should expensive or sentimental belongings. Extra attention to the security of your personal effects should be practiced until both parties demonstrate sufficient proof that the other can be trusted. This proof would be demonstrated through a history of mutually respecting each other's belongings (such as food, furniture, hygiene products), adhering to privacy needs and assisting with shared responsibilities like chores and rent payment. It is vital you and your roommate practice mutual respect to avoid a breach of trust.

Your autism symptoms might amplify personality traits or needs (e.g., rigid adherence to a schedule, eating the same things repeatedly, sensitivity to loud noises or temperature). There are quirks to everyone's personality, and when people live together these idiosyncrasies are magnified. Even a person you have known for a long time or someone you know well may surprise you once you live together. Roommates may be messier or cleaner than anticipated, they may sleepwalk or snore or they may use your things without asking. The first step is to expect that you will learn new things about a roommate (both good and bad) and to determine which issues should be addressed and which should be accepted.

Positive Qualities in a Roommate

Everyone needs to decide which qualities are most important when choosing a roommate. While no one person will be perfect, some qualities are desirable, some are manageable and others are simply not acceptable. Below is an example chart that you can fill in outlining the qualities you do and do not want in your roommate.

Most desirable	Manageable	Not acceptable
Polite Quiet	Social Late sleeper	Smoker Throws parties

Roommates or Friends?

Being someone's roommate does not mean he or she is automatically a friend. Plenty of people who know each other and work well together as roommates do not socialize with one another outside of the home, nor do they develop a friendship. In fact, you might prefer this kind of roommate relationship, as living with a very good friend can have its downsides. For example, even the best of friends need a break from one another. When roommates are also best friends and spend a great deal of time together they can easily get irritated with one another. When you live with a very good friend its natural to spend quite a bit of time with one another, making it difficult to separate "friend time" from the alone time we all need and expect at home. Roommates who live together and socialize together must communicate about their needs for rest and privacy at home (see Social Script 7.2). Sometimes, to preserve a friendship, living with a trusted individual who is *not* a best friend is a better choice.

SOCIAL SCRIPT 7.2 COMMUNICATING YOUR NEED FOR ALONE TIME

"I really like being your roommate and hanging out with you, but like I mentioned when we first moved in together, I really need time to decompress and be alone. I don't want you to think I am being rude or do not like talking to you and stuff. How about I signal to you that I need time alone by going into my room and closing the door or when I put my headphones on? You can interrupt me if there is something important to say, but otherwise, we can talk or hang out when I come out of my room or take off my headphones."

Roommate Agreements

In communal living situations (e.g., college dorms, shared housing) roommate arrangements are usually facilitated by a set of guidelines created by the system or homeowner and adhered to by the roommates. These agreements allow for a discussion of your personal preferences and individual needs like privacy, noise and temperature and some guidelines about the division of housework. Any roommate situation can benefit from the development of roommate agreements. In the absence of set guidelines, you may wish to develop a roommate contract, or set of agreed upon guidelines, that outline expectations and attempt to prevent misunderstandings and disagreements. Some roommate agreement items include: cleaning, meals and cost of purchasing food and home goods. Additionally, some thought will need to be given to noise level preferences and individual schedules (are the roommates morning or evening people?). Some issues, like whether to recycle and whether to allow overnight guests or parties, are issues that must be discussed prior to moving in with a roommate. Roommate agreements are best discussed in a casual conversation, and then formally drafted, with both parties getting a copy of the agreement. Chores will also need to be addressed. Talking to your roommate about expectations for maintaining a clean and organized environment is an important step in this process. Other resources (and expenses) like heat and air conditioning should be discussed with regard to usage and payment. A roommate agreement should cover logistical matters as well as personal preferences for the shared space.

Establishing a roommate agreement that is signed by all parties is a good way to manage expectations. While the agreement is informal and not legally binding, developing a list of shared standards for behaviors and roommate responsibilities can help prevent problems and create a safe and comfortable living space for everyone. It is important that you have a strong understanding of your own individual needs and are comfortable advocating for these needs independently. Understanding and planning for these needs in advance will make it easier to discuss them with your potential roommate. The figure "Roommate agreement chart" highlights some of the most common roommate responsibilities and provides some guidance for drafting a roommate agreement.

Roommate agreement chart	
Who's doing what:	**Weekly chores:**
~~Zach~~/Chad/Sam	Dishes
Zach/Chad/~~Sam~~	Take out the trash
Zach/Chad/~~Sam~~	Clean bathroom (mirror, toilet, tub, floors, sink, etc.)
~~Zach~~/Chad/Sam	Kitchen (sweep, mop, wipe counters)
Zach/~~Chad~~/Sam	Living room (vacuum, dust, tidy up)
Zach/~~Chad~~/Sam	Outside clean up
Bills are due:	
Rent: due on the 1st/$500 each	
Electric: due on the 16th/? (will be posted on the 10th)	
Cable: due on the 10th/$75 each	

Roommates should discuss the items in the figure "Roommate agreement checklist" in detail and draft an agreement about how to address them in advance of moving in together.

<u>Roommate agreement checklist</u>

Cleaning

- How does each roommate define clean?
- How will dishes be managed? Wash after each use or schedule for dishwashing?
- What are the rules about emptying the dishwasher or putting dishes away?
- How often will roommates clean bathrooms? Together or taking turns?
- Who is responsible for cleaning the kitchen? How often? How thorough?
- How often will the roommates clean the living room?
- Who will take out the trash, and how often? Will the roommates recycle?

Socializing with guests at home

- Does either roommate have concerns about overnight guests? What will the rules be about overnight guests?
- How will young adults share common space when guests are over?

Communication

- How will the roommates discuss conflict?
- What is the preferred method of communication between roommates (e.g., email, in person, text, phone call)?

Shared personal items

- Who will supply a television and video games in the common area? Can everyone use them? What hours are acceptable?
- Which roommate will provide appliances (e.g., microwave, coffee maker)? Are there any guidelines for their use?
- Will the roommates be sharing food? All food or just some items? Are there any dietary allergies?
- Does either roommate have concerns about sharing cooking supplies? Is anyone keeping kosher?

- When individuals run out of cleaning products, how will they be replaced (e.g., taking turns, group fund for cleaning supplies)?

Preferences

- Is either roommate an early riser or a light sleeper? Does one roommate wake up immediately after the alarm goes off while the other presses the snooze button repetitively? What are the proposed quiet hours?

- What are music preferences if played in common areas, and preferred volume levels? Do you prefer to listen to music privately with headphones on?

- How will the roommates set the temperature for the shared space?

- What areas are private and what areas are shared?

Safety

- What is the evacuation plan for emergencies?

- Who should be contacted in an emergency concerning young roommate?

- What are the expectations for locking doors, both shared and to each bedroom?

- If there are guns in the home, where are they located and how is safety addressed?

**SOCIAL SCRIPT 7.3 DISCUSSING RULE
VIOLATIONS AND NEGOTIATING ADJUSTMENTS**

Leslie's roommate Sydney has a habit of playing video games late into the night on high volume. The living room, where the gaming console is kept, is right next to Leslie's room and makes it hard to sleep. Since both girls work early on weekday, they'd originally agreed to shut off the television at 10 pm.

"Hey Sydney, I'm having trouble getting to sleep, because the game is very loud. Originally we'd agreed to shut down the television (including games) at 10 pm. I was thinking about some solutions that would allow you to still play, but help me get some much-needed sleep. Would you mind wearing headphones while playing after 10? This way, you still get to play, but I get to sleep."

When it comes to setting up privacy in a shared living space, you and your roommates can designate rooms in the house to have different privacy levels.

- **Completely private**: Bedroom.

- **Semi-private** (i.e., private when in use, but a shared space): Bathroom.

- **Shared space with limited privacy expectations**: Living room, kitchen, porch/balcony

The figure "Apartment with noted privacy zones" depicts a visual breakdown of a shared apartment and the designated privacy "zones."

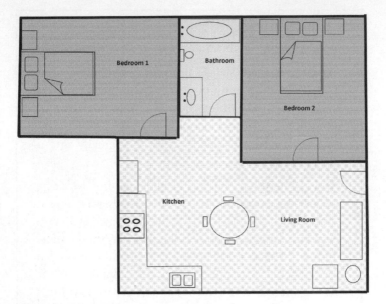

Private space	Private/shared space	Shared space
• This is your private space. Just as you expect others to respect your privacy, respect theirs as well. Only enter others' private space when invited.	• Keep space organized and clean. • Close the door to signify you need privacy. • Formulate a schedule for usage of shower/bathroom, especially at busy times (morning before work).	• Establish guidelines and have a clear understanding of the expectations of the others you live with. • Be considerate of guidelines that you have established like temperature setting, quiet times and shared items.

Apartment with noted privacy zones

Summary

Transitioning to adulthood, especially to living independently, requires advanced thought and coordination. Transitioning to living with a roommate involves extra care and communication to avoid missteps. By utilizing the checklists and roommate questions, drafting a roommate agreement and learning to recognize your triggers, you can more positively approach adulthood with increased confidence.

References

Anderson, K. A., Shattuck, P. T., Cooper, B. P., Roux, A. M. and Wagner, M. (2014) 'Prevalence and correlates of postsecondary residential status among young adults with an autism spectrum disorder.' *Autism 18*, 5, 562–570.

Aud, S., KewalRamani, A. and Frohlich, L. (2011) *America's Youth: Transitions to Adulthood.* Report of the US Department of Education, National Center for Education Statistics. Report no. NCES 2012-026. Washington, DC: US Government Printing Office.

Furstenberg, F. F. Jr. (2010) 'On a new schedule: Transitions to adulthood and family change.' *The Future of Children 20*, 1, 67–87.

Rigler, M., Rutherford, A. and Quinn, E. (2015) *Independence, social and study strategies for young adults with autism spectrum disorder: The BASICS college curriculum.* London: Jessica Kingsley Publishers.

Chapter 8

Household Safety

TOP SAFETY CONCERNS

★ Weather emergencies.

★ Driving.

★ Fire.

★ Emergency planning.

★ Interacting with police.

While our son was away at a college support program, snow and extreme cold caused the college to shut down for more than a week. Since the support staff for the program managed a lot of his banking, he and other students were left with minimal funds. Some students from out of town had to manage at their college apartment without any support for several days. (Sherri and Marty, parents of a son with ASD)

Another aspect of developing independent living skills is household safety. Most people think of their home as a place of refuge where they feel safest from dangers around them. Unfortunately, the truth is that each year millions of people are injured in their own homes. A report[1] showed that injuries within a person's home resulted in an average of 21 million medical visits per year. Although these statistics can be scary, it is important to remember that many household injuries can be easily *prevented*.

It is important for you to be familiar with basic safety. Knowing what to do and where to go in an emergency, taking preventative measures to ensure safety and recognizing potential obstacles will help you prepare for potential safety concerns. Considering the safety tips and techniques in this section will help you prepare for potential hazards and arm you with solid advice. The more understanding you have around basic safety, the better prepared you will be for emergencies and accidents.

The goal for safety drills and evacuation plans is to teach you to recognize danger and respond quickly and appropriately. You will benefit from *very specific* and *exceptionally clear* procedures, especially because the commotion—loud noises, panic and fear, lights, smoke, etc.—can be overwhelming to the sensory system and disrupt rational thinking (see Tip 8.1).

---

1   Center for Injury Research and Policy (2008)

TIP 8.1 Helping individuals with ASD understand safety protocol

☑ Use visual aids or videos to accompany the policies and procedures, especially emergency procedures.

☑ Explain sequentially in a step-by-step procedure (best accompanied with a visual).

☑ Use repetition to learn the procedures.

☑ Practice the procedures (live drills) at regular intervals.

☑ Discuss several scenarios and the accompanying response.

Developing a Safety Plan for the Home

Young adults with ASD have a tendency to think logically and rationally. This inherent strength will prove quite helpful when developing a safety plan for you. While a neuro-typical person may react emotionally to an emergency situation, because of your ASD symptoms, you are more likely to follow an established plan. Knowing this, you can approach basic household safety with confidence and maintain safe independent living skills through the development of routines. Fortunately, adherence to routine is a strength in people with ASD, and you will be less likely to stray from the routine (regardless of the emotional or situational stressors you may experience). In addition, your adherence to a routine could be helpful in supporting others like roommates or family members who are around at the time of the emergency. However, sometimes in emergency situations, things don't go according to plan, and you will also need to be somewhat flexible. Everyone should have a plan B, especially in the case of a fire. When developing a plan, it is important to include an explanation of *why* a specific action is being taken. This way, you are able to apply this reasoning to an *alternative action plan* when the scenario changes. An example of this benefit can be explained by Patrick, who utilizes routines daily for safety and is comfortable with the safety protocol he needs at home:

> I'm very safety conscious—I always unplug my lamps when I leave my room, and I double check that kitchen appliances are off before leaving. I even have a towel by the door to block smoke if there's a fire at home and carry my shoes down the stairs so I don't fall. (Patrick, young adult with ASD)

Safety Alerts

One way that you can prepare for potential safety issues is to be aware of the variety of safety alerts made available to all citizens. Safety alerts come from many different sources. These sources include the weather channel on local television, the internet and radio announcements. Other safety announcements could come from campus text alerts, landlord alerts or police scanning apps on smartphones. It is important to keep in mind that regardless of where a safety alert originates, it should always be taken seriously.

Taking precautions at home is essential, but you cannot prevent every safety issue. Sometimes emergencies happen suddenly and you must react quickly with the resources available. When it comes to issues like weather, fires and even burglary, you should be aware of both precautionary and responsive safety practices. Having emergency kits ready for bad weather and being sure to lock doors are both precautionary safety measures, while crawling to a safe exit during a fire is a responsive safety measures. You can utilize your tendency for following routines and thinking logically as you seek to address emergencies both through preparation before they occur and response if an emergency takes place (see the table below).

Precautionary and response safety actions		
	Precautionary	**Responsive**
Fire	Place a smoke alarm on every level of the house.	Crawl on floor to avoid smoke and evacuate immediately.
Burglary	Keep doors locked.	Call the police immediately.
Weather	Keep flashlight next to bed.	Take shelter.
Driving related—daily	Manage distractions.	Keep cell phone put away.
Driving related—police interaction	Follow all road rules.	Pull to the side of the road and provide requested documents.
Driving related—accident	Be aware of other drivers.	Assess for injury and call 911.

Weather-related Emergencies

While no one can prevent or prepare for *all* emergencies, an understanding of emergency preparedness for things like weather can pay off in the long run. The very nature of an emergency is sudden, so it is hard to know when/where/how one will occur, which could be very unsettling for you.

Planning responses before the emergency can help reduce your anxiety about weather-related emergencies. You should learn to take advantage of media alerts and take preparatory measures such as those listed below.

- Obtaining home/renters' insurance (e.g., flood, tornado, earthquake).

- Having a safety kit in the home: batteries, emergency cash, first aid supplies, flares, copies of your driver's license) (see the figure "Home emergency kit").

- Ensuring that an emergency supply of water and some cash are on hand.

- Having a generator or emergency power supply.

- Stocking up on candles and matches, and having a flashlight next to the bed.

When it comes to weather safety, you should be mindful of the weather patterns in your area and recognize signs of severe weather in order to plan effectively for potential weather-related issues. When weather calls for you to take cover, in a basement or other shelter, it is helpful to have a battery-operated radio or weather radio to track the weather and alerts.

Preparing for weather-related emergencies is a safety responsibility, no matter where you live. Knowing your region's common weather events can help you prepare for the most likely situations (see the figure "Regional weather patterns"). For example, in the US, someone on the coast of Florida would need to recognize potential for hurricanes and prepare accordingly, while this would be unnecessary for someone in Kansas. Likewise, someone in Massachusetts would need to be aware of snow-related weather concerns, while their Florida counterpart would not. Being aware of the potential impacts of different regional weather emergencies helps you prepare for the most likely weather-related issues.

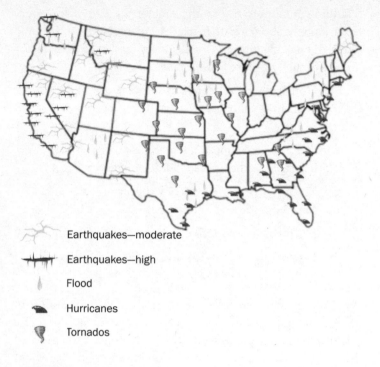

Earthquakes—moderate

Earthquakes—high

Flood

Hurricanes

Tornados

Regional weather patterns

Weather advisories come in specific levels. The figure "National Oceanic and Atmospheric Administration's weather warnings" lists definitions from the National Oceanic and Atmospheric Administration's National Weather Service in the US (2009). Weather stations may use these terms when describing weather patterns, and it is important know the characteristics and implications of each and how they differ from one another.

National Oceanic and Atmospheric Administration's weather warnings	
1 "Monitor the weather"	When a **watch** is issued: Although the weather forecast is still uncertain, the risk for bad weather has significantly increased across a period of time.
2 "Be aware"	When an **advisory** is issued: The weather circumstances are likely to be an inconvenience and may continue to be dangerous, but are not as serious as when a warning is issued.
3 "Be prepared"	When a **warning** is issued: Hazardous weather is occurring or imminent or is very likely and conditions pose serious threat to life and property.

Whether or not you are living independently, you should have a plan for the weather-related emergencies that may occur that includes specific plans for home, work, school or other frequented areas. Sometimes there are established procedures for responding to weather in an organized way, and these procedures are often practiced, like tornado drills at schools. It is best to practice your personal emergency plan in a similar fashion. Practice and repetition is the key. It may also be useful to practice the routine with different contingencies; for example, when practicing seeking shelter, discuss what you would do if the shelter were blocked. Tip 8.2 offers additional considerations for weather-related emergencies.

TIP 8.2 Considerations for weather-related emergencies

KNOW Your Weather!

Some geographic regions experience particular types of hazardous weather. For example, some parts of the northeastern area of the US experience significant winter weather, like extremely heavy snow. There are higher rates of tornados in Kansas and Oklahoma, whereas in coastal locations like the Carolinas and Louisiana you need to know what to do in the case of hurricanes. Remember, before you travel to a new place, you may want to familiarize yourself with the procedures related to these types of situations. See the figure "Regional weather patterns" to examine the potential weather patterns for your area.

KEEP an Emergency Kit Ready!

Emergency gear can minimize the time it takes to take action when every second counts. Create a kit and store it where it can be accessed quickly, like under the bed. See the figure "Home emergency kit" to see what a well-stocked kit includes.

PLAN for Pets!

Be sure to plan—and practice—for how you will ensure your pet's safety during emergencies. Some shelters do not allow pets, so also consider how you, or someone else, will care for your pet if you are ever displaced from your home.

PLAN for the Location!

Weather preparation does not stop at home. You should have a plan for home, work and the car.

PLAN Together!

If you have roommates or housemates, planning for weather-related emergencies should happen together. Each person can be responsible for a part of the plan, and you should practice your roles together.

KNOW the Different Types of Preparation!

Review safety tips for each *specific* kind of weather disaster including thunderstorms, flash flooding, earthquakes, tornadoes and hurricanes.

- Candles
- Blankets
- Extra batteries
- Flashlight
- First-aid kit
- Medication
- Canned food
- Can opener
- Bottled water
- Matches

- Radio (wind up or battery powered)
- Knife
- Duct tape
- Rope or paracord
- Protein bars
- Cell phone
- Cell phone power bank
- Supplies for pets
- Other

Home emergency kit

Fire

> The element in our oven caught on fire once. It helps to have a plan, so my family and I came up with one and have a window ladder[2] to use from the upstairs rooms now. (Jordan, young adult with ASD)

In addition to weather, you need to consider fire safety precautions and procedures. Unfortunately, fire hazards are a very real threat, causing over seven billion dollars in property damage in the US in 2014.[3] In addition to causing property damage, a fire can cause serious injury to people and pets. Therefore, it is highly important to develop a solid plan for prevention and management of fires.

Planning for safety and practicing the following fire prevention tips can help you decrease the potential for a devastating loss due to a fire in the home. Fire prevention is a necessary topic of discussion as you move towards independent living. Fires can be prevented by being responsible and cautious and respecting the power of fire. There is no guarantee that a fire will not happen, but taking Tip 8.3 into account will lower the likelihood of experiencing a house fire.

---

2   A window ladder is a portable ladder that allows one to crawl down safely from an upstairs window.
3   Federal Emergency Management Administration (2015)

TIP 8.3 **Fire prevention**

☑ Install smoke detectors on every level of the home.

☑ Keep flammable items at least three feet away from any heat source.

☑ Turn portable heat sources off when leaving the room.

☑ Never leave frying/grilling/boiling food unattended.

☑ Keep burning candles out of reach of children or pets.

☑ Check electrical cords for fraying or breakage.

☑ Store matches and lighters in a safe location.

Fire Safety Plan

If a serious fire occurs, it is critical that everyone knows how to get out of the house or building as *quickly* and *safely* as possible. You may have heightened sensory sensitivities that could make fires even more overwhelming. Smoke can cause irritation to the eyes, nose and mouth, while fire alarms can cause intense sensory overload to the ears and eyes due to the loud noise and associated strobe lights. Consequently, in response to fires and fire alarms, you may be inclined to hide, freeze or panic rather than exiting the building. Hiding is a dangerous response. *No one should hide during a fire*—the goal is to exit the building as fast as possible. Once you have a plan, practice it often. The first and most important goal is to get out and get away from the fire. This is a lot easier said then done. Fire and smoke are equally dangerous and can block exits to the building. Smoke hoods can be part of a safety kit and can protect the wearer from smoke and other toxic gases while they work to escape the fire. Practicing this plan is essential, as Aaron mentions below—it should become like muscle memory!

> All plans go out the window when something like that happens. It's muscle memory. It's not so much about schedule or doing something over and over again. Going over an escape plan repeatedly when something happens you will just do it because its part of your routine. It's muscle memory. (Aaron, young adult with ASD)

Plans should include at least *two* options for evacuation. If the primary plan becomes too dangerous or risky based on the location of the fire, the back-up plan can be a lifesaver. For example, if the primary plan is to evacuate out the back door of the apartment and the fire is isolated in the area by the back door, you should plan to use an alternative exit. Every plan should include a meeting place for all parties outside of the dwelling that is a safe distance from a possible fire. Everyone should agree on this spot in advance and remain there until the authorities and emergency response crew arrive. This will be how you confirm that all parties were able to exit the building. Time is critical during a fire. While it can be tempting to want to "take" important items with you, remember that every second counts and that death from smoke inhalation is a very real concern. Material items are just that—they can be replaced; humans cannot!

In addition to home fires, you should be prepared for fires or other safety concerns at work and school or other places you frequently visit. Most people have seen an evacuation plan either in the hallways of a school/hospital or on the back of a hotel door for emergencies like fires. These plans use a red line to indicate possible safety routes out of the building and highlight all exits. It is a great idea to pay attention to these signs upon entering a new location. You could review a sign visually or even take a picture of it with the camera on your smartphone. Sometimes important fire-related information is communicated over intercoms, like in some movie theaters and airports. Patrons should pay close attention to any emergency-related announcements and ask for clarification if they were not able to hear or understand what was said.

> If there were a real fire at work, I wouldn't know what to do. Even though we have had drills, I'm still unclear about what I would do. In addition to managing the unannounced nature of the fire drills, my job at a nursing home involves helping other people reach safety, too, so there's a lot of risk involved. (Patrick, young adult with ASD)

In the workplace or at school, the safety procedures may not be very organized or well communicated, so it is important to inquire about the procedures for emergencies. In some places of employment, such as hospitals or schools, employees may be responsible for directing others out of the building. If this is a requirement of your job and you are uncomfortable with this expectation or not confident in your ability to respond in this way in an emergency, it is vital to communicate this to your supervisor. Safety is a public concern, which is why many drills and evacuation plans are in place across different environments in the community. When the procedures aren't discussed thoroughly or individuals are not given the opportunity to practice the plan, things can go awry. It is important to have a plan no matter where you are and to practice it (see Tip 8.4).

TIP 8.4 Responding to fires

☑ Fire extinguishers are great for small fires, but do not attempt to fight a fire yourself. Use the extinguisher to make a safe path and *get out*.

☑ Remember that fires can spread quickly, making it difficult for an individual to escape without a plan.

☑ Set up smoke alarms throughout your home, especially near rooms where you and your roommates or family members sleep, so you'll be awoken in the case of a fire.

☑ Test fires alarms and change batteries every six months. Most have an alarm that sounds when batteries are low.

☑ When you consider your fire safety plan, consider strategically placing safety tools near window and doors in your home; for example, leaving a hammer by the window in case you need to break it to escape or get fresh air. You may want to place a portable ladder in upstairs rooms to help you safely evacuate if the door or stairs are filled with smoke/flames.

☑ Smoke inhalation kills more people in a fire than the actual flames. Individuals are advised to stay low to the ground and crawl to an exit. Air masks are also helpful.

☑ Closing doors to isolate the fire can help prevent it from spreading. If you touch the knob to any door and it is hot, do not open it because it is likely that the fire has reached the other side of the door. Find another way out!

☑ If you find that flames are on your body, do not panic and run. Remember the fire safety rule: "Stop, Drop and Roll."

Burglary

> In the dorms, random thefts occur frequently. People are too trusting and leave the doors opened/unlocked. I try to put myself into the mindset of a criminal. I think, "How would a criminal see this?" Then I try to do things to prevent that from happening. (Dave, young adult with ASD)

More burglaries occur in the Unites States than any other country in the world.[4] According to www.safewise.com, four burglaries happen every minute in the US, which translates to one burglary every 15 seconds.[5] It is scary to think about a stranger entering your home or car and going through your personal effects, but burglaries do occur and need consideration as a potential safety concern, especially if you are transitioning to living alone. The National Crime Prevention Council suggests that people do not advertise that they live alone and that they call local law enforcement authorities if they feel threatened.[6]

Until you know your neighbors and your neighborhood better, adjusting to independent living requires extra caution with strangers. Children are often given a rule at home: "Don't open the door for strangers." This rule was set into place to prevent people with bad intentions from accessing the home, taking valuables and/or threatening the safety of the people in the home. The same rule should apply when you live independently. Sometimes, a stranger at the door is harmless, like a young student selling candy for a school fundraiser or a neighbor seeking her lost dog, but sometimes the person at

---

4   www.crimereports.com
5   Chianis (2015)
6   National Crime Prevention Council (2008)

the door has bad intentions. As a rule, not letting strangers in your dwelling is strongly suggested. You should use cameras or peepholes to identify individuals at the door and determine whether or not you should respond (see Tip 8.5).

TIP 8.5 Meeting new neighbors

While it is often customary for people to welcome a new neighbor with baked goods or a simple introduction, it is not recommended that you invite them in. It is perfectly acceptable to have a brief conversation at the door and get acquainted without letting them in. It is also unwise to tell people information that could possibly tempt or facilitate a break-in, such as, "I just bought a brand new television" or "I work overnight shifts at work."

Burglary Prevention

The impact of burglary can be devastating. In addition to losing valuables, the stress of having to interact with law enforcement, negotiate with insurance companies and replace essential items quickly can overwhelm anyone, but these added stressors could be especially difficult for you to handle. Although no one likes to think about intrusion and theft, it's an essential safety element to consider. Fortunately, there are several preventative measures you can take when it comes to theft and intrusion. Locking the doors can prevent burglaries. This applies to your home vehicles, tech items and wallets/purses. The doors should be locked when leaving the home or getting out of the car and locked again when reentered. If you keep your bike outside of your home, use a bike lock to attach it to a bike rack or other permanent fixture. It is also wise to avoid leaving valuables in plain site (in the car or home), as they could tempt would-be thieves. You can also dissuade potential burglars by having someone check on your home and car while you are out of town or by using lights with a timer to give people the impression that you are home.

Another preventative measure is installing a home (and/or car) protection alarm system. Alarm systems vary in price and options, but the fundamental role of the alarm system is the same. They are designed to alert you when your home is entered by anyone who is not expected to arrive. Most systems have a key code that you enter when you leave or arrive, arming or disarming the system. On some systems, you can even utilize surveillance video and activate the security system from a digital device, like a smartphone. A yard sign alerting people to the security system can be displayed to deter potential burglars. Even less expensive strategies can be employed to deter criminals, such as maintaining a well-lit property through the use of outdoor and motion-activated lights. Even having a dog—especially one that barks—can help prevent a burglary.

While these precautions can deter theft and intrusion, there are no guarantees. If someone forcefully enters your home or car, the situation changes and other steps must be taken (see Tip 8.6).

TIP 8.6 Steps to follow if you are burglarized

☑ Immediately contact local law enforcement.

☑ Take note of missing items and write down all of the information you can about them, including a physical description and all identifying features you can think of, like identification numbers, or something you added to the items personally, like your name or a colored case.

☑ Contact insurance agency.

☑ If someone tries to enter the home while it is occupied, *immediately call for help*!

Insurance

Having homeowners' or renters' insurance can help with replacing property in the event of theft or damage. Having insurance can be useful for more than just case of a burglary. Major and minor car accidents, weather-related disasters and fire emergencies are typically events that different insurance plans cover. There are insurance plans for all types of situations including: medical coverage, homes (owners' and renters' insurance), cars and even for specific things like electronic goods and jewelry. Insurance comes with varying levels of coverage and protection. Documenting the theft with law enforcement can help authorities and insurance companies work to obtain stolen goods and or replace items. Sadly, many items that are stolen are either damaged or never found, making it important to have safeguards in place in the form of insurance. If you are living independently you will need to obtain insurance for your home and possessions. Insurance should be viewed as a safety net and included in a monthly budget. It is important to research and speak with several insurance companies before choosing one and ensure that all items are properly covered. Comparing and choosing insurance can be overwhelming. You should ask family and friends for recommendations or use comparison websites, which can be found with a Google search (see Tip 8.7).

TIP 8.7 Before getting insurance

☑ **Do your research**. Find the insurance company and plan that is right for you. Sometimes you can get reduced rates by purchasing several types of insurance plans from the same provider. Sometimes it makes more sense to have different companies for different plans. The point is shop around and shop smart.

☑ **Take stock of belongings and take photos** to verify the existence of high-priced items like stereo equipment, televisions, collectibles, artwork and jewelry.

☑ **Investigate the replacement cost** for all items in the home to estimate how much coverage is needed.

☑ **Estimate the amount of money needed if you are displaced**, for temporary housing, food, etc. This will allow an insurance company to build these expenses into your plan in the event you need to place a claim.

Driving and Using Public Transportation Safely
Driving
Driving is another skill that develops over time and with experience. In their book, *Expect a Miracle: A Mother/Son Asperger Journey of Determination and Triumph,* David and his mother Sandy discuss how they approached driving in a stepwise process. She talks about the challenges of driving, as noted in the excerpt below:

> We opted for a two-step driving process, much like we handled the college transition. Freeway mastery would follow after a year of comfort and experience with local city driving...Dave was a careful driver, and he was self-assured in traveling to places he had driven before...New destinations or the need to follow directions still stressed him. He was not comfortable splitting his concentration between the actual driving and the lookout for landmarks or signage. To solve this dilemma, we would take David on trial runs; for example, if he was invited to a party, he would practice the route in advance...and [after having] his questions answered...proceed by himself for the actual event. He would subsequently add the new location to his growing list of independent trips. I imagine he will eventually become more adventurous and skilled, but in the meantime, safety was our priority.[7] (Sandy Petrovic, young adult with ASD)

Independent living, for many young adults, involves driving or taking public transportation. It is necessary to ensure that you can get to and from work, school, appointments, the grocery store and social gatherings safely. You might feel comfortable driving and have the financial stability to maintain a vehicle

---

7   Petrovic and Petrovic (2014)

and insurance and therefore choose to drive to and from various destinations. Conversely, you may choose to take public transportation, which might involve first taking a walk to a bus stop or the subway line. Either way safety should be considered.

> I took an extra year before getting my driver's license. Driving is scary because there are a lot of potential dangers on the road. I still have some trouble reading other people when I'm driving but I try to notice things like if they are driving too fast or if they are following too close, and I'll wave them by me. It helps to be clear-headed and think logically. (Neal, young adult with ASD)

Due to the symptoms of ASD, you are more likely to make errors while driving, due in part to levels of attention, visual-motor integration, motor coordination and visual acuity required by the driving experience.[8] It is important to minimize driving errors and ensure the safety of yourself as the driver and other bystanders. You can work to develop strategies that strengthen driving abilities in the area of multitasking, acclimating to the noise levels on the highway, developing better hand–eye coordination, increasing attention to detail, monitoring reaction times and adjusting speed for road conditions. Practicing these skills will lead to more confidence and safer driving.

Practicing driving can help you become more accustomed to the rules that govern driving. In addition, planning for the unexpected while driving can help people respond to challenges as they occur in the moment. Distractions should be kept to a minimum—things like texting or playing music loudly, especially when first driving, should not occur.

---

8   Classen, Monahan and Wang (2013)

As well, accidents are more likely to occur when young adult passengers are in the car,[9] as they are an added distraction. Although you likely want to show off your new driving skills to all of your friends, it is best to get some experience of driving alone first.

You will benefit in many ways from extra practice when it comes to driving. Practicing the rules and laws of the road makes drivers aware of the broad range of items requiring attention while behind the wheel (e.g., other drivers, construction, accidents, stop lights, road and/or weather conditions, etc.) and can help limit distractions that might occur. There are plenty of opportunities for distraction on the road. It may take intensive time and practice to become comfortable behind the wheel of a car and learn the rules, both written and unwritten, of the road. Beyond driving school, there are other tips that help increase driving efficacy:

- Practicing with someone who can give experienced advice and feedback.

- Gaining experience with a trusted and competent driver can improve your skill level and confidence, particularly for advanced driving skills like parallel parking, driving in reverse, shifting lanes and highway driving.

- A driving companion for individuals who struggle with focus and directions can help navigate or coach an individual through unexpected driving challenges.

- Practicing with an experienced driver is a great way to help you learn how different functions of the car work, like using windshield wipers in the rain, learning how the car responds to different speeds and

---

9   Centers for Disease Control (2015)

roadways, using cruise control or understanding car warning lights/alarms.

Unfortunately, practice does not always make perfect. While driving education and practice can increase the odds of a safe driving experience, there are many unexpected situations that cannot be rehearsed. For example, swerving to avoid a semi-truck's blown tire while driving 70 mph on a highway cannot be practiced in reality. Thankfully, some video games and virtual websites exist to help new drivers practice. One such website is Virtual Driver Interactive.[10] It presents drivers with virtual simulations including texting and driving and dangerous weather conditions—teaching drivers how to react safely without facing the real (and potentially deadly) consequences. Simulation allows you to practice what to do if a hazardous situation should present itself, giving you the best possible chance of surviving or avoiding a crash. It is impossible to guarantee that others are making safe choices, and therefore practicing defensive driving should be done virtually and in reality as well. By being a defensive driver— not making assumptions about other drivers, expecting other driver's to make mistakes (i.e., follow too closely, make sudden turns without signaling or weave in and out of traffic) and maintaining a safe distance between cars—possible accidents can be averted. Aside from having strong driving skills and practicing defensive driving, there are other safety strategies to consider while driving, like the use of cell phones, poor driving conditions, emergency car kits and what to do in case of accidents and interacting with police.

---

10 www.driverinteractive.com

Cell Phones and Driving—A Dangerous Combination

> It took me some time to be comfortable driving, and I didn't get my driver's license until I turned 21. There are so many distractions on the road that I try to limit the distractions in the car, too. I don't listen to the radio or use my cell phone, and I keep both hands on the wheel. I have to be focused when driving because all the sensory factors make me even more anxious. (Patrick, young adult with ASD)

Drivers traveling via car should keep a cell phone with them in case they need to call for help, have access to alerts, check for weather updates or find alternative routes, but there are safety concerns with using a phone while driving. Phones are great for emergencies but are also an added distraction. Sending text messages and reading them while you are driving can be fatal. No text is so important that it cannot wait. A few seconds of glancing at a phone to read a text while driving is sufficient to cause an accident. In fact, recent figures report that cell phone use while driving leads to 1.2 million accidents per year.[11] Calls while driving should only occur in emergency situations and only via Bluetooth or other hands-free technology.

Fortunately, many phones are equipped to work with technologies like Bluetooth to make hands-free communication easier, and some are even voice activated, making communication on the road a completely hands-free experience.

---

11 National Safety Council (2013)

POOR DRIVING CONDITIONS

Driving conditions can also contribute to safety concerns on the road. In bad weather, drivers can experience weather delays and/or unsafe driving conditions. Road visibility can deteriorate quickly due to rain, snow or fog, therefore it is critical to use extreme caution, slow down or even consider stopping and waiting for the weather to pass. For example, you should stop when driving conditions are not optimal and "wait it out" at a safe place, away from the roadside if possible (to avoid further accidents) and exit off the main street taking refuge in a well-lit parking lot. Sometimes, pulling to the side of the road may be the only option but it can be risky in poor driving conditions because cars will be driving very close to the edge of the road. If you do have to pull over on the roadside you should keep your emergency lights flashing and make sure to pull far enough off the road to avoid collision with oncoming traffic. You should never exit out of the car on the road side, but should crawl over to the passenger side of the car to exit.

> I use a couple of mantras when driving in bad weather. "Half the speed, twice the distance," and "Easy on the gas, easy on the brake." These sayings remind me to be safe on the road. (Hikarih, young adult with ASD)

VEHICLE EMERGENCY KITS

Vehicle emergency kits are always a good idea. Drivers often rely on a family member or auto service to help them out if an emergency occurs. Unfortunately, that is not always an option. Cell reception may not be reliable in inclement weather, preventing you from contacting family, friends or emergency responders in a timely manner. The inability to contact help in an emergency situation would cause anyone a great deal of stress. Planning ahead and including vehicle emergency kits in all cars will help relieve stress and address a driver's needs in emergency situations (see the figure "Vehicle emergency kit").

In addition to the items in the figure "Vehicle emergency kit," other useful items include flares, which can be placed around the car to alert other drivers, and protective gloves to wear while changing a tire. Weather conditions will also inform your vehicle emergency kit. For example, for folks who live in the desert, it may be wise to keep a sunshade for the windshield to protect against the heat if your car breaks down or is stalled for a long period of time. Conversely, if you live in a snowy area, items like cat litter, a spare shovel and hand warmers could help combat the snowfall and cold. The most important action in any emergency is to try and remain calm until help arrives.

ACCIDENTS HAPPEN

Accidents happen. When an accident happens there are specific steps that must be followed. First, the driver of both vehicles should attend to injuries and call an ambulance immediately if injuries are apparent. As well, the drivers should call the police to file a report (this is the protocol required by insurance companies). Once the police arrive, they will ask everyone involved about the accident and issue any citations that are warranted, in addition to writing a report. Drivers should exchange contact information with one another and also exchange insurance information. Some insurance companies offer kits with guidance about what to do in an accident (see Tip 8.8).

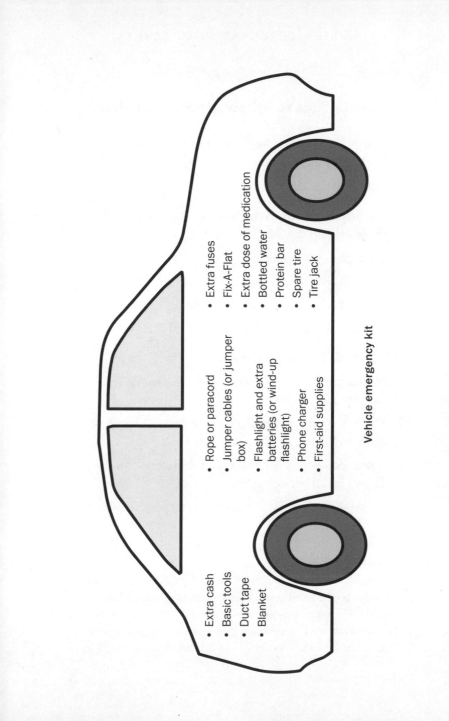

- Extra cash
- Basic tools
- Duct tape
- Blanket

- Rope or paracord
- Jumper cables (or jumper box)
- Flashlight and extra batteries (or wind-up flashlight)
- Phone charger
- First-aid supplies

- Extra fuses
- Fix-A-Flat
- Extra dose of medication
- Bottled water
- Protein bar
- Spare tire
- Tire jack

Vehicle emergency kit

TIP 8.8 Tips to follow after an accident

☑ Call 911 if anyone is hurt—do not move a person who has been in an accident.

☑ Get off the road.

Take a picture of the vehicle, the crash site and other pertinent evidence:

☑ Damage to your vehicle.

☑ Accident location.

☑ Photo of other driver and their vehicle.

☑ Do not make any statements to the other driver.

Collect the following information:

☑ Name, address, phone number of the other driver (if they are able to speak).

☑ Make, model, year and license plate number of the other driver's vehicle.

☑ Name, policy number and phone number of the other driver's insurance company.

Interacting with Police

One of the things we worry about when our son drives is how he might handle an accident or being stopped by the police. He keeps everything he needs—car information, registration and insurance information—ready just in case, and he has a plan with information about what to do, but the key is he needs to remember to use it! (Marty and Sherri, parents of a young adult with ASD)

IN AN ACCIDENT OR ON THE ROAD

If you are in an accident, you should cooperate with the police and collect the badge number, name and police report number for the accident. In addition to accidents, you could also be pulled over by a police officer while driving for a number of reasons including: if you are speeding, if a parking brake or taillight is blown out, if you have expired tag or if you are driving erratically. Sometimes police have random checkpoints to check for drunk driving, which requires that you either talk with the officer to answer questions or get out of the car to perform some gross motor skill tests like walking along a straight line and touching your finger to your nose. The officer may shine a light in your face to gauge eye movements or pupil dilation or to detect intoxication. The officer may speak with quick demands and with a firm and intimidating demeanor. When interacting with law enforcement, it is important that you always remain polite and compliant and have a firm understanding of your legal rights.

BEHAVIOR PROTOCOLS

There are behavior protocols to follow when interacting with law enforcement. Some of these behaviors may not come naturally for you because of your autism symptoms—for example, police often expect people to look them in the eye as a sign of respect, which is often hard for people with ASD. Police also tend to give a number of directions to people at the same time, in rapid succession. Because you may have some difficulty with receptive and expressive communication, it may take you longer to process these directions. This delay in responding can be misinterpreted as disrespect, impairment or non-compliance with a police officer (see Tip 8.9).

TIP 8.9 Interacting with police

☑ Do not get out of the car unless instructed to do so by the officer.

☑ Keep calm.

☑ Give the officer the requested documents and In Case of Emergency (ICE) card.

☑ Tell the officer you have autism.

☑ Wait patiently while the officer checks your information in their vehicle.

☑ Follow directions and ask for clarification.

In responding to an interaction with a driver who had ASD, Officer KM offered the following reflection.

> Tell drivers to be sure to disclose their diagnosis and the side effects of their medication to the officer. In this situation, the driver was arrested for a DUI because his medication made his eyes jump and his field sobriety tests were difficult for him because of balance, the instructions were too detailed and he never asked for clarification and expected perfection with his performance. Had he told me in the beginning, he may have saved himself a night in jail. Drivers need to understand that this is not necessarily a get-out-of-jail card, but it is more valid if the card has a doctor's signature and contact information. Ultimately, they still need to cooperate and answer the questions, relax and not overthink the instructions given. It is OK to ask the officer for clarification or for a demonstration. (KM)

Given this advice and the potential difficulties in interacting with police it is wise to carry an In Case of Emergency (ICE) card. This ICE card identifies the individual as a person on the spectrum and lists associated challenges (e.g., lack of eye contact and delayed processing of multiple-step directions). The card also includes emergency contact information for parents or guardians, medical information, hospital preferences and medications. Simply handing this card to the officer at the same time as you present your driver's license could save a lot of confusion and future complications (see the figure below).

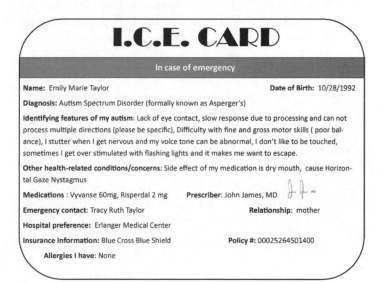

In Case of Emergency (ICE) card

Alternatives to Driving

If you choose not to drive, there are many alternative methods of transportation. You can walk or bike if you live close enough to the destination. One perk of these methods is that you are getting exercise at the same time! Public transportation is a popular way for many people to commute to work and to run daily errands. Some cities have excellent public transportation including subways, trains, light rails, buses and trolleys. These public transportation systems are often intricately designed, like the subway system in New York City, but most follow set routes and have designated stops along these routes. Most of these systems have apps for iPhone or Android smartphones that allow you to navigate the system expertly and identify expected arrival and departure times. Whether you ride your bike, walk or use public transportation, being mindful of safety is important.

PUBLIC TRANSPORTATION SAFETY

Being safe while using public transportation is largely a matter of awareness. As with any safety plan, being prepared is vital. Preparing for alternate routes in the event of mechanical issues or line blockages and identifying safe areas at each stop on the line can be a part of the planning process to begin using public transportation safely. Taking public transportation can be a way to get from place to place, often cheaply and quickly, but if you are traveling alone it is important to use precautions and consider some safety and etiquette tips (see Tip 8.10).

Public transportation safety

- Know your stop
- Be attentive and aware of the surroundings
- Listen to announcements
- Keep a little extra cash on you just in case
- Keep track of all your valuables
- Bring hand sanitizer
- Go with a friend when possible

TIP 8.10 Safety considerations for taking public transportation

☑ Take a little extra cash for another bus or subway ticket, just in case.

☑ Keep track of all your valuables and do not use them while taking public transport (i.e., hide your phone, computer, purse/wallet, etc.).

☑ Be attentive and aware of the surroundings so as not to miss the stop.

☑ If someone bothers you notify the driver or attendant.

☑ Keep a charged cell phone with you at all times.

☑ Follow the posted rules and policies.

☑ If there are open seats allow space between you and other people for privacy.

☑ Listen to announcements and ask someone or the attendant if you were unable to hear what was announced).

☑ Bring hand sanitizer and wash your hands after using handrails to stairs and in buses and subways to prevent the spreading of contagious illness.

☑ When chatting with others watch for non-verbal social cues (i.e., limited responses, focused attention elsewhere, headphones in ears, etc.) and respond accordingly.

☑ Keep important numbers in your phone and written down in your wallet or personal bag.

☑ Due to the crowded nature of public transportation in certain cities and times of day, you may want to avoid use during peak times (i.e., rush hour, sporting events, concerts, etc.).

☑ Use extreme caution when using public transportation late at night, and try to make it to your destination before midnight or go out in groups of two or more late at night.

BIKING SAFETY

Biking is a popular option if you decide not to drive. However, there are some inherent risks when people on bikes share the roads with motorized vehicles. Bike commuting is often popular in larger cities, which may have specific biking lanes to promote safe travel, but these lanes are not always provided in smaller cities and towns. If you are traveling by bicycle, be aware of and follow the rules of the road. Just as there are specific rules for automobiles, there are also specific rules for people riding bikes. It will be important for you to be aware of both sets of rules to be able to bike safely (see Tip 8.11).

Bike Safety Kit
- Water
- Mirror
- Reflective tape
- Reflective lights
- Pant band
- Lock
- Helmet

TIP 8.11 **Biking safety**

☑ **Wear a helmet!**

☑ **Use hand motions to designate turns and stops**. You should research the specific motions that are used in your town by cyclists on the road.

☑ **Attend a bike safety course** if your community offers one. Some of the classes actually offer a riding tour, where the rules of the road are demonstrated in a group with a leader.

☑ **Get to know the rules of the road** that drivers follow, even if you don't drive. This way you can anticipate the actions of drivers more accurately.

☑ **Bring a lock** to secure your bike when you get to your destination

Summary

Independent living is about more than managing a home. Household safety, like weather awareness, fire prevention and response, burglary and driving and public transportation are all considerations that must be addressed. The majority of young adults have a desire to live independently and to do so requires some planning and preparation. To be able to prepare for safe, independent living, you must think about the potential for emergencies before they occur and develop response strategies for how to manage emergencies should they happen at home or on the road. Establishing a foundation of safety strategies for independent living can be the key to less stress and more productivity and happiness!

References

Centers for Disease Control (2015) *Teen Drivers: Get the Facts*. Atlanta, GA: Centers for Disease Control. Available at www.cdc.gov/motorvehiclesafety/teen_drivers/teendrivers_factsheet.html, accessed on 2 November 2015.

Chianis, A. (2015) *The Safewise Report*. Salt Lake City, UT: SafeWise. Available at www.safewise.com/blog/8-surprising-home-burglary-statistics/, accessed on 2 November 2015.

Classen, S., Monahan, M. and Wang, Y. (2013) 'Driving characteristics of teens with attention deficit hyperactivity and autism spectrum disorder.' *American Journal of Occupational Therapy 67*, 6, 664–673.

Federal Emergency Management Administration (2015) 'Home fires.' *Ready Campaign*.

Hodges, N. (2015) Home Safety Program. Available from www.nationwidechildrens.org, accessed on 4 February 2016.

National Crime Prevention Council (2008) *Robbers are Equal Opportunity Criminals*. Arlington, VA: National Crime Prevention Council. Available at www.ncpc.org/resources/files/pdf/neighborhood-safety/robbers-are-equal-opportunity-criminals.pdf, accessed on 2 November 2015.

National Safety Council (2013) *Annual Estimate of Cell Phone Crashes 2013*. Itasca, IL: National Safety Council. Available at www.nsc.org/DistractedDrivingDocuments/CPK/Attributable-Risk-Summary.pdf, accessed on 2 November 2015.

Petrovic, S. and Petrovic, D. (2014) *Expect a Miracle: A Mother/Son Asperger Journey of Determination and Triumph*. West Conshohocken, PA: Infinity Publishing.

Chapter 9

Keeping Track of the Dough

Safe and Smart Money Management

> I learned about money management when I was younger.
> I had my first credit card when I was 13, and I had to
> learn how to manage money, pay bills and keep track of
> my private information. (Neal, young adult with ASD)

Learning to manage personal finances independently is
essential to financial safety. Responsibilities for financial
independence include paying your own rent, saving for
the future or having cash on hand for parking or public
transportation. Managing finances in a safe and thoughtful
manner requires planning, organization and preemptive
safety steps. Establishing bank accounts, being mindful of
account privacy and realizing the importance of budgeting
for all monthly needs are essential parts of your financial
responsibility. This chapter offers tools and strategies to
facilitate the transition to independence through responsible
money management.

Security Concerns

Account Safety

Most people use a bank to house their money and pay for items through an account. There are multiple types of accounts including checking, credit accounts, savings accounts and accounts just for business. You can also use money transfer services like PayPal and others that transfer funds between your account and businesses or individuals. Setting up a bank account typically involves meeting with a bank representative to discuss options and then reading and signing various documents that detail your arrangement with the bank. Once an account is set up, methods for accessing the money include accessing it in person, at the bank, indirectly via an ATM card or via online banking. To access the account, you must show identification or use an identifiable password, like a debit PIN code. This PIN code is also needed whenever you make purchases with a debit card or withdraw cash from an ATM.

Because of the security concerns around account numbers and associated codes or PINs, great care should be taken to keep this information private. Allowing someone access to your passwords, PIN codes or account numbers gives them access to your accounts and the money in them With this information, someone could make fraudulent purchases or, worse, steal your financial identity. If identity theft occurs, thieves can overspend on your account, which can cost you in insufficient funds charges or ruin your credit by opening an account under your name and then allowing the account to become delinquent. These financial missteps can have long-term negative consequences on your financial well-being. While you might trust someone's intentions and have no problem sharing your financial information, this is never a good idea. Unless the account is joint (i.e., shared with another person) or a family member, you should not share passwords, PINs or account numbers with anyone (see Tip 9.1).

TIP 9.1 ATM safety

☑ Never share your PIN number with another person.

☑ Do not make your PIN number your date of birth or other easily identifiable number.

☑ Do not write your PIN code in plain site.

☑ Shield the ATM screen from strangers when entering your PIN code.

☑ Be aware of your environment.

☑ Don't count your money at the ATM.

Money Management

You should monitor your spending via bank statements or real-time online access (on a computer or via an app). This includes monitoring information about your purchases and current balances and ensuring that all charges are correct. Conducting regular reviews of bank and credit card statements alerts you to fraudulent charges and unanticipated bank fees. Many banks also offer alerts for spending; for example, charges over a predetermined amount (for example $50) prompt a notification to the owner via text alerting them to the charge. This is a great way to get alerts about spending and let you know if someone else is using your card. Keeping money safe requires vigilant monitoring of your accounts and an awareness of account activity at all times.

Shopping Safely Online

Many retailers offer online methods for making purchases. Buying things online can be convenient (as items can be easily ordered via the web and delivered right to your home or business, reducing the need to go to the store). After a few orders, some online retailers even start to predict your purchases, making the experience highly convenient. Technology is quickly evolving new ways to make people's lives easier. You can even order and pay for a pizza to be delivered without making a phone call!

Despite the convenience of online ordering, you need to approach these purchases with caution. When considering purchasing something online, ensure that the websites checkout method is secure (i.e., going through an encrypted site). Websites like www.staysafeonline.org, https://epic.org/privacy/intl/eu_data_protection_directive.html, www.cba.ca/en/consumer-information/42-safeguarding-your-money/65-

staying-safe-online, and www.communications.gov.au/what-we-do/internet/stay-smart-online offer a wealth of information about staying safe when making online transactions, like how to ensure that the site is legitimate and how to protect your personal information. When ordering online, it is always important to log out or shut down a browser before leaving the computer on which purchases are made. Third-party pay options like PayPal offer secure payment platforms that keep your credit card information private, allowing you to transfer money to individuals and purchase items on eBay and multiple consumer websites; best of all the service is completely free.

Storing Credit Card Information

While storing information for future use can be convenient, you should be careful only to store account or credit card information if you frequent a specific retailer and are certain that the retailer has a *secure checkout system*. Credit card information should *never* be stored on a computer that is used by other people. Most websites will offer some kind of statement that lets you know how information will be stored. It is critical that you monitor your credit card statements to detect any fraudulent purchases and contact the credit card company right away if you see a charge that is unfamiliar.

Budgeting

Keeping track of spending is beneficial for many reasons. A budget plan that outlines the funds necessary for daily/monthly living is essential for all adults and provides structure to their financial organization. Knowing how much money is available for a certain period of time (e.g., a month or a year) is the first step in creating a budget. Running out of money, or not having enough money to cover expenses, can lead to serious consequences over time, including missing payments on bills, having service interrupted for utilities, being evicted from a rental apartment or home and damaging your credit. Poor credit can ruin opportunities for getting further credit and being approved for an apartment or home and can even impact the annual percentage rate (APR) you get on car loans, house loans and credit cards. When you are just beginning to manage your finances you need to build up some financial reserve until you better understand your *true costs*.[1] Following a weekly or monthly budget, and not spending your reserve, ensures that you have enough money to get through the month.

A budget plan involves analyzing income (total amount you have to spend in a given period of time, like one month) and expenses (the various purchases and services required over a period of time, like new clothes, rent and utilities) in order to determine a plan for spending. The basic premise of a budget is to determine how total income can be divided to ensure all expenses are paid, using approximate spending costs. The figure "Sample monthly budget" provides an example.

Budget: Monthly income $2000	
Expenses	Cost
Rent	$650
Gas/car maintenance	$150
Groceries	$200
Restaurants	$100
Home supplies/maintenance	$50

---

1   The actual cost of living versus the projected or budgeted cost.

Utilities (electricity, water, cable and internet)	$250
Fun money	$150
Savings	$200
Total expenses: $1750	

Sample monthly budget

When arranged in a pie graph (see the figure "Monthly budget"), it is easy to identify patterns in spending. In this example, the person spends most of their income on rent, while setting aside a relatively small amount of money for entertainment and fun.

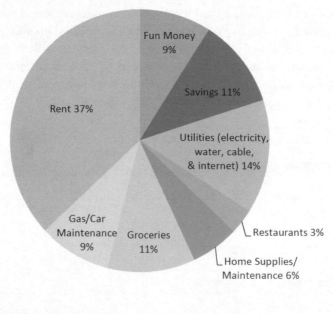

Monthly budget

Developing an accurate budget takes time and some trial and error to ensure accuracy and consistency. In addition to income and expense categories, budgets need to include more specific categories so that spending is accurately tracked. For example, transportation is a broad category. If you own a car, you may need to sub-categorize for gas or car maintenance and insurance. Alternatively, a category for the cost of public transportation should be included if you do not drive. Emergency funds should be included in the transportation category for cabs or a car service like Uber or Lyft in case of breakdowns, construction or other issues that make public transportation unavailable. Maintaining financial stability and adhering to a budget will allow a newly independent you to save money for the future and for travel or a down payment on a house.

Finally, an emergency fund is essential. Once a determined monthly cost is developed, the rule of thumb is to save at least three months' worth of expenses in case of an emergency. While the budget is a *prediction* of monthly expenses, it does not plan for the unexpected.

An emergency fund provides a safety net against unexpected financial needs and will keep people from having to rely on credit cards and loans, or family, when a crisis occurs. When it comes to being responsible with money, saving some income for those unexpected events can reduce stress during an otherwise stressful emergency.

Here are a few examples of sudden costs you might incur when transitioning to independent living.

CONSIDERATIONS: POTENTIAL UNEXPECTED EXPENSES

- **Travel:** For example, young adults need to book a flight to a different location to visit a sick relative.

- **Home/car repair:** For example, a major car repair need.

- **Medical bills:** For example, having to pay to spend the night in the hospital after an accident and insurance co-pay for each subsequent doctor visit.

- **Job loss:** For example, the company that employs young adults must lay off ten employees and you lose your job.

- **Children/pets:** For example, a dog gets sick and needs a round of expensive antibiotics.

Summary

Being a responsible and independent young adult includes keeping yourself safe physically, emotionally and financially. With the use of technology to monitor financial standing with various account types, it is much easier to keep yourself on an established budget. Creating a budget and sticking to it is a vital step in financial security. While using the internet to manage financial issues, it is imperative to keep your personal information protected to avoid potential pitfalls such as money theft or identity theft. By creating additional rules for living within you means and protecting you financial security, you can follow these rules to create a stable financial life for yourself.

Index

INDEX